My Extraordinary Family

THE GOOD, THE BAD, AND THE MIRACULOUS

To: Lucia
GOD has blessed me with His Love truly
Through You truly
ONE of His cherished
VESSELs.
Victoria M.
AKA
Elaine (your sister)

Victoria M.

ISBN 978-1-0980-9722-6 (paperback)
ISBN 978-1-0980-9723-3 (digital)

Christian Faith Publishing, Inc.
832 Park Avenue
Meadville, PA 16335
www.christianfaithpublishing.com

Printed in the United States of America

To my siblings who have shown much love
and kindness to me over the years.

Appearances

Now here on February 10, 2020, I want to tell you about the *family* I grew up in during the 1940s to 1950s. We were, for all to know, very middle-class to upper middle-class. It would depend on who was viewing us. I am certain some would say we were privileged, while others would say we didn't quite make it through to upper middle-class status.

What is most remarkable to me is that we were so "good-looking." Everything positive you could say about a family would seem to fit. Successful father, exemplary stay-at-home mother, four lively and well-attended siblings—perfect number: two boys and two girls. They have seemingly very normal rivalries—truly good looking, even well-behaved foursome.

Oh, we were normal—maybe too much of the "good-lookingness"? I doubt most people would have questioned this *wonderful* (looking) American family.

The address of my growing up was 1211 Boundary St. The town was a strange one in western Pennsylvania.

Add to this a regular church-going and the families of Cal; my Papa; and Leo, his brother (that would be my Uncle Leo) on the short list of contributors to local church. Papa and his brother, with their families, attended a Catholic Church of more than a thousand families; they competed to be the highest donors. In this case, the parish published a list of total contributors by name and amount.

Papa—a leader among men, one of the supervisor of Rollers, an elite group of steel industrialists who not only headed up crews of men in steel production but were father figures to the rank-and-file members. There is a newspaper article entitled "Leave it to the "M" Boys." It featured Cal; my Papa; Leo II; my uncle; and Leo; my grandfather. The article pointed out the Jones and Laughlin Steel Corporation credited this father-and-son(s) team with being instrumental in building what was then one of the largest mills in the county.

But it didn't end there. These three also ran departments largely responsible for the company's success. Built on the Ohio River north of Pittsburgh, it stretched close to ten miles along the riverbank. The mill my Papa ran as supervisor of Rollers was known as the four-teen-inch mill and was the only one of its kind. In the industry, it was titled "the university of rolling mills."

In the house of my growing-up years, it seemed we had something akin to perfection. Mama was a stay-at-home mother, who was a true homemaker—very creative and attentive. Even though I didn't know much about working mothers since they were not part of this landscape, I was acutely aware of how important it was to have her there waiting for us and waiting on us most all the time. I didn't think we were spoiled; I would learn what a dichotomy I lived much later.

Mama had a college degree when few of her generation were able to attain that goal. She taught piano before she married Papa. It was also reported she played piano for theaters when they showed silent movies.

I clearly remember hearing the works of Bach and Beethoven and Chopin, to name a few, being played in our home on the baby grand piano—a gift from our Papa to Mama when I was a very young child.

Papa was gifted in math and engineering without benefit of college. He was a natural in his chosen profession. He also exhibited talent in a much different expression. He taught himself to tap dance and appeared in shows as a song-and-dance man. I now believe some of that ability came out of his Irish heritage. He also entertained family and friends in the living room of that Boundary St. house in that dirty mill town in western Pennsylvania.

I never doubted my Papa was a strong and courageous defender of the family. Although, when I think of it, I don't actually know how I knew that. He was without question a good provider. All those growing-up years, I don't remember any sense of insecurity, and we heard of the many times Papa would intervene in other families' situations and he would rescue members out of dire circumstances. He seemed heroic in many of these family crises.

Calling to mind a member of Papa's crew who had a drinking problem and whose wife would call Papa to save her from her husband's abuse. I remember Papa taking that young man under his wing. His problem was alcohol. Papa hired him to paint the house and, of course, he continued to work as a crew member at the mill where Papa was supervisor. I don't remember many more late-night trips to save his wife from her abusive drunken husband once Papa took him under his wing.

Getting back to Papa, he was a tall lanky young man with big ears and a happy—not handsome—face when Mama first met him. You could imagine he was arrested in looks at about fifteen years old. But as he grew older, he developed a mature, somewhat-distinguished facial structure. However, that delightful Irish mug remained—a little boyish with a strong hint of manliness I always loved. He was a tease and would disarm even the most sophisticated with his creative humor.

There is the family lore that as a single man making good money in the mill, he had a wardrobe so impressive it gained him the name The Count among his peers.

I feel certain this Irishman charmed our mother before any chemistry attracted her to him. One of Papa's business associates exclaimed at a social gathering, "Tell me, Cal, how did you, an ugly Irishman, get such a beautiful wife?" I think he took pride in that fact.

This quite charming Irishman, who entertained his children with funny antics that captivated and brought smiles and often outright laughter, was a down-on-the-floor kinda playful Papa. The three of us would pile on him and he would let us take him down, but not before the squealing, skirmishing, and finally tumbling into a full-on heap of children—with him at the bottom.

In the category of quirkiness, a few of my Papa's behaviors seemed strange to me and, I assumed, to the rest of the family.

One was his fear of windows that were uncovered; he would always make sure the blind over the window he was facing as he sat at the dining room table was drawn. He was adamant about this. You could sense a real fear behind this. And although we kinda joked about this one, it too was no joking matter when you examined what was going on for Papa.

He would never leave the first floor of our two-story house without opening the closet door in the downstairs entry hall. It was as if he was convinced someone could be in there. And when he was working the 4:00 p.m. to midnight shift at the mill, he would stop and turn on the overhead light in each of his children's bedrooms—this was a check to make certain that we were all in our beds safely. There would be some context for these things much later in my life.

At some point in my childhood, I sensed that my dear Papa was not respected by the rest of the family, and I took it upon myself to defend him at every turn. This may have been more imagined than real, but I certainly believed he needed a defender. I was the one who always took his side. Whatever development-in-compassion happened, I definitely knew it when relating to my Papa. I really believe I was his favorite. As history played out, this reality took on a very different meaning.

And now Mama.

Mama would always intercede for her children in any situation we found ourselves—especially with an authority that was, to our way of thinking, unjust. If Sister so-and-so called us out for disobeying her, we would report to Mama who would listen to our side of the story and immediately go into action. She would right the wrong. She was very skillful and ultimately disarmed the nun/teacher. There was never any retaliation against any of her children; that's how good Mama was.

Another arena in which she excelled was pleading our individual case, persuading authorities to allow us to enter places that seemed impenetrable without her manipulation on our behalf. She single-handedly got my brother into a college that, without her influence, would not have been opened to him.

She did not make enemies, but in the community, there were those who did not like her because she was very pretty and was perceived snobbish. The way I saw it, she was always compassionate (it didn't matter who you were) and would help wherever and whenever she could. She never seemed condescending. That is not snobbish.

Now I see that she was a bit introverted and could be perceived as snobbish, I guess.

She quietly assembled a scrapbook that contained photos and stories of wealthy families always presented in a good-news light. She admired this class of people in our country.

My mama would have been a good therapist. She listened to us and never seemed to judge. You could tell her anything. She would ask questions and give advice that always made me feel better and made me feel I was understood and forgiven. Sometimes there were perimeters such as, *You need to go to confession.* We were Catholic, and therefore, her absolution was sometimes conditional. We needed to go to a higher power.

She was gifted, intelligent, loving, sensitive, very merciful, and devoted to her family in every possible way.

She was a good neighbor and friend. Mrs. T. lived next door, and her oldest son was killed in World War II. This woman's grief was profound. Part of her coping was to call my mama nearly every day for many months and cry and pour out her grief, including talking about her son, the circumstances of his death, and whatever else she found helpful to process the pain.

I remember it happening over a long period of time, and it was incessant. Mama always stayed with her on the phone until Mrs. T. was finished for that day only to take it up again the next. There may have been times when they got together, that would not surprise me, but I clearly remember those calls.

She ministered to a drug-prescription-addicted neighbor. I now believe she was trying to be helpful but didn't really understand what the need was. You could say she meant well.

Mama was a flirt. I still don't really know how conscious she was of her part. What was amazing was that Papa never noticed. It all seemed harmless at the time.

During a family outing, a day at the races, I became aware that a man who appeared to be close to my age (I was in my forties) was definitely flirting with my mama, not me.

As a couple, my mother and my father modeled a beautiful picture of sacrifice. Mama loved classical music, and Papa was an avid sports fan. Admittedly, Mama was better at this; she deferred to his sports and became a true follower, especially of football teams, as time went on. Papa, on the other hand, finally went to a concert with her—once and that later in life.

She never complained about his golfing, bowling, skeet shooting, or other activities he enjoyed on his time off. Incidentally, he was better than average at all these endeavors.

Rose

ose was my sister and the firstborn of four. She was a child of the depression, born in 1927, and that explains some of the differences in our family experiences. She has told me experiences of deprivation, remembering wearing clothing far too small and not appropriate (i.e. a cotton dress that was too short or too tight) in winter.

She has vivid recollection of being left to babysit the three of us when she was just twelve years old, overwhelmed by this responsibility and by the behavior of us three. We were often mean and threatening toward her. On one occasion, she was left for a weekend with no backup and no communication.

I have a very vague memory of this. I understand how frightening that must have been. She was truly on her own, no backup, and little communication with our parents. Goeff—our brother who was five years younger than Rose—was the original ADHD child, as our mother would tell it. He had some aggressive behaviors and truly ruled his siblings with an iron fist which he used regularly on us, especially the area of the upper arm which he managed to punch sharply if we dared to stray from his rulings. He was capable of whipping up the young ones to do battle against our poor sister as she attempted to keep us safe and keep the peace. Our parents did not know the magnitude of her assignment. Rose never told.

One incident Rose clearly recalls is when we attempted to push her out of an upstairs window. That would have been a two-story drop no doubt, resulting in serious injury or more. Somehow she was able to fend us off. I have no recollection of this, but that doesn't mean it didn't happen. My sort of flashback recall confirms the wild-and-threatening behavior.

An epiphany at age twelve, Rose saw the road ahead as intimidating. Pondering life at twelve was not something I did. Coming in the middle of the pack is just not the same. Could it be that some of the experiences she had contributed to this pondering? Or, as she will tell you now, she really never liked life.

In her case, Rose at that early age had already concluded that life was at best difficult and at worst more than she could handle—a rather overwhelming birthday for a preteen. You could believe that fear may have entered in at that time.

Rose grew into a lovely girl with auburn hair and hazel eyes. She had the mark of the Irish: lovely to the eye and, well, just very pretty. Vivacious and fun, but underneath it all was a realist bordering on pessimist of great magnitude. She was my hero (we would have said heroine in those days), and she resembled our mother—not quite petite, but definitely not tall like our dad. She attracted male attention with her appearance as well as her friendliness.

She managed to be a really good daughter, be a protective big sister, and ultimately be a star in the family.

There was the episode that is now a most-important family legend and, incidentally, is true. Rose was five years older than our brother Goeff (aka Sonny, aka Red). While Goeff was quite young and vulnerable, some smart-aleck, tough older girls accosted him, wrapping a scarf tightly around his neck; Goeff was traumatized.

When Rose found out what had happened, she hunted down the perpetrators and—fueled by the anger she was holding against them—confronted them and let them know: "If you ever try anything like that again, I'll get you." From all accounts, they were intimidated and ran to their parents with part of the story.

Not long after, the parents appeared with the principal in Rose's classroom and mistakenly tried to put my sister in her place. Rose was having none of it. In front of the entire class, Sister Bernadette (the school principal) queried, "Why did you act this way toward these girls? You had better apologize."

To which my sister replied, "I won't, but you can tell your girls if they ever do anything to hurt my brother again, I will come after them."

Then there was the persona Mama and Papa promoted as far back as I can remember. Rose was not only a hero; she was extrovert-extraordinaire. The buzzword of that generation, or at least in our household, was *personality*. The better yours was, the greater your worth. This was communicated very effectively. I remember feeling somewhere between "I'll never be like her" to "I am very jealous of her." I believe parents fall into this without realizing how it feels to their children. There must be a better way.

Suddenly, or so it seemed to me, Rose began to rock the boat. She was *so popular*, and until Gene came on the scene, everything was great.

They met in college and began to date a perfectly normal sequence; however, not so fast. This was serious, and he was a cripple. At twelve years old, I didn't really perceive anything wrong with him. In fact, I thought he was a very nice person. It was not so with Mama and Papa. They may have believed he was a nice person but just not for their daughter. Aside from shattering their dreams of her marrying some near perfect person, I would hear arguments from them: "He will never be able to carry groceries or, worse yet, pick up your child."

Gene had been stricken with polio as a young child and spent time in an iron lung. In the 1940s, this was the lifesaving treatment for the disease. He managed to survive and recover well enough to walk using canes.

Rose tells a touching story about the first time she saw him walking into the classroom. Struck by his handicap, she thought to herself, *I bet he doesn't have a friend in the world*; but noting his strength, her heart definitely responded. As you hear her tell the story, you know that this was without doubt love at first sight.

The next time she saw him, they were taking a test in that same classroom. His flirtation was sliding a paper across the desk for her to see the answers—by any other word, *cheating*. That did it; Rose was totally hooked; unfortunately, they both failed the test. They didn't get caught—just plain failed the test.

So back to the family. Parent's cajoled, tried threats, bribery, and much persuasion—nothing worked, but this is what I remember as the younger sister. I was watching this family struggling in a way I had not seen before. Anxiety and arguing was the order of most days. And finally, after months of wrangling, wedding plans became the order of the day. Mama switched gears and began to work her magic to make it all very lovely. And it was.

During this amazing time in the family, Rose began to student-teach. The wedding was memorable because all the elementary students in her class at that time came and, for me, because I was maid of honor. Incidentally, they were a good-looking couple.

Then came the move. Gene was offered a job on the other side of the state, Philadelphia; Rose was pregnant; and Mama was heartbroken because Gene decided to take the job—and they moved. Rose would still tell you she would have gone anywhere her husband needed or wanted to go. And he would go where the opportunity to provide for his family would take him.

Mama, on the other hand, would not support them in any way. Rose was pregnant and was somewhat at risk. She was Rh-negative; this was her first pregnancy, and that blood type could complicate matters. This was the 1950s, and medicine had not discovered a way to lessen the danger of her condition.

I remember visiting her a few weeks before the baby was to be born. I was struck by her joyful anticipation in spite of the fact they were in unfamiliar surroundings with little opportunity to be introduced to the community. Being with her husband and with child seemed more than enough for Rose.

Then came October and labor and delivery. We got the phone call announcing the birth and, shortly thereafter, announcing the serious condition the newborn was in. They named her Mary, and she lived for three days.

Although Rose and Gene moved back to Aliquippa, shock and grief ruled the day and a dark depression was with my sister.

Then Cal was born, and the family that Rose and Gene would parent began to take shape. Three more boys later, they settled into a lively lifestyle that, in some ways, embodied what a family of boys should look like. They were unbridled in the activity they maintained. Their dad—Gene—at one point arranged to have a pool table brought into the dining room of their wonderful roomy house. That house seemed to fit the needs of a healthy family of growing boys. Formal dining room table gave way to a pool table, and they gathered to enjoy the manly art of shooting pool.

If I am not mistaken, it was also a gathering place for their friends and, to some extent, kept the four engaged at home.

Gene also encouraged and delighted to support his active sons in most all their endeavors, especially physical activities (football and the like). I am certain they would tell you they were not in any way hindered by the fact their dad was handicapped. Truth be known they likely did not perceive him that way. He was a positive, uplifting person and imparted a can-do attitude. He was a quintessential optimist, and if you haven't noticed or figured it out, Rose was the pessimist.

However, Rose was the perfect mother of four boys. She did not find disorder, bordering on chaos, disturbing. She was not interested in keeping house, as most women would interpret it. She focused on the important things—the development of her sons in becoming men for one.

She was a professional woman, a teacher. She returned to teaching at a point in the marriage where financial needs dictated it. In a peculiar way, this served a purpose in Rose's life. Since she was not particularly interested in the domestic arts, most especially cooking, being a working mother could sometimes act as a cover.

A story she tells about her husband in their early days of their marriage—Gene kept hinting at wanting a potato as part of his dinner, and Rose kept dodging this, using every excuse she could possibly come up with to avoid cooking potatoes. To tell the truth, I don't know if the potato issue ever got a right resolution. Suffice it to say,

Rose was not a cook and didn't even pretend to try. She was a home-maker, not a housekeeper.

Then there was the night Rose got the phone call we all dread and pray never comes. "Mrs. C., your husband has been in an accident. He was hit by a car and is in the hospital." This is enough for anyone, but for a man whose legs were already greatly compromised, this could have very serious consequences. He had suffered broken bones in his leg that was stronger (but certainly not strong), as well as other injuries.

Gene was accustomed to navigating obstacles all his life, but this could forever change that. Once again, that strength that rose up in my sister in the past when tragedies and challenges struck was there to get her through. Gene was in a complete body cast. He was discharged from the hospital but needed much care. For many weeks, going into months, he was in a hospital bed in the living room of that wonderful roomy house. Rose now became his nurse 24-7.

After months of recovery, Gene returned to the world of work. The nature of the work Gene engaged in was often political—from president of chamber of commerce to working with federal funding in urban renewal. From small town in western Pennsylvania to mid-sized Ohio town, many times he was at the mercy of the political office holders of the day. Therefore, his work/job could end based on the change of power.

So there were good times and bad. At one of the lower points in all this, Rose and Gene faced economic reality that was about to cost them their home. Every attempt to straighten the course of the ship had failed. Then one warm spring day, in the midst of their personal trial, there came a storm. A real storm—a tornado that ripped their house apart; the house that was about to go into foreclosure. The good out of this storm became a rescue enabling them to begin again.

During one of the good times, the family had traveled to Florida for a vacation. They enjoyed that family vacation and became enamored with Florida. Armed with the insurance money from the destroyed house in Ohio, they found their way to a little town in northern Florida and settled down. Rose is still there. In some ways, she is living happily ever after. At age ninety-three, she still sees much of this thing called life as inexplicable. But to this day, she and I enjoy each other on regular weekly phone calls, during which she keeps this little sister out of la-la land and in some kind of reality.

Her youngest son lives with her, and she would tell you, "He takes very good care of me."

There is one wonderful story Rose tells that sort of says it all when describing her and her family.

When her second-born son Eugene was born, they brought him to her; and she will tell you that when they put him in her arms, he gave her a dirty look. How's that for a bonding experience?

On their anniversary, not long after moving to Florida, she and Gene celebrated at a local restaurant. After returning home, Gene was seated in his favorite chair, and Rose was talking to him as she walked through the room. She was telling him how much she appreciated the love he had given her all throughout their marriage and before.

As she turned to look at him, she noticed he was slouched in the chair and she said, "I guess this is boring since you fell asleep." But suddenly she realized he was not sleeping. He had had a heart attack and died.

When someone truly loves you, they literally set you free; and so long as that commitment to love doesn't end, you remain free and appreciative and reciprocal.

Rose would tell you she was loved that way by her husband.

Goeff

On May 20, 1933, baby boy Goeff was born to Cal and Marie. I would like to believe joy was the state of the family on that day. This child would be referred in the parlance of the family many years later as a (the) child of destiny. He was beautiful. Like his older sister Rose, he was red-haired; however, his was a strawberry blond—hers was auburn—and he had blue eyes.

He was challenging in his infancy. Mama would tell how she would bathe him frequently just to calm him. Behavior science had not yet gathered information to understand ADHD.

At age two-and-a-half, with my father in the hospital for a ruptured appendix, little boy Goeff underwent surgery for a collapsed intestine. The doctor commented to my mother that doing surgery on this little boy's body was like working on a fine watch.

My mother was sorely tested with her husband on one floor of the hospital and her child on another. She would tell me years later how the doctors told her my father's condition was very serious, and he may not make it. When I think of her response, it encourages me but, later in my life, would confuse me. She had a very interesting faith. She confessed to me that she knelt beside my father's bed in the hospital and, in her brokenness, commended him to his heavenly Father. He recovered.

And so did my brother Goeff. He was like a little brother among the neighbor boys—only often it looked as if he was their leader, not the other way around. We have photos of the neighbor boys, and they bear a striking resemblance to *The Little Rascals*.

Admittedly there are some blank years, ones where I don't have clear memories of my brother. Not sure why that is, but I do remember that we lived approximately two miles from the St Titus Elementary School, and Goeff insisted we run the entire way or else. Either I ran until I couldn't run anymore, or I went by myself the whole way. He ran, and I ran. I ran until I couldn't anymore. I never figured out if he ran all the way, but to this day, I believe he did.

Goeff taught me how to skip school and spend the day in a nearby woods. Kinda spooky when we found evidence of someone living there in the middle of the woods. He also was the one who uncovered truths, like there was no Santa Claus and babies came from mommies' stomachs. Don't recall anything about how they got in there.

And then there was the day while our brother Ed had scarlet fever and the family was quarantined. We devised this game, quite certain Goeff was the author. It was the spring of the year, and we were allowed to go outside so long as we didn't leave our property.

After Goeff coached me on climbing out on the second-story roof, he set up the rules to this new game. It involved our sister Rose. When she was "it," she would lock us out of the house, and we were to find a way in. We never got to the point where we were "it" because after Rose locked us out, Goeff found this obscure basement window. It was located on the side of the house that had no doors, no access. The window swung inward from the top and, as with most basement windows, was near the ceiling with about an eight-foot drop to the basement floor.

It was unlocked and was surely our way in for points to win the game. Only thing is there was a wooden post that prevented Goeff's head from going through the opening of the window. Yes, he was literally hanging above the basement floor unable to get himself back up and out.

We panicked and began screaming, but this was a big house; no one was answering our screams. It may have been minutes, but each second counted here; and just as I was getting ready to hurl a rock through the neighbor's window, Mama and Rose showed up in the basement near the window. This was only the beginning of the rescue.

Now I know the logistics of the matter: Rose stood on a chair that just happened to be nearby and held Goeff by the legs so that he would not choke, while Mama sawed off the wooden post, letting the window swing up so that Goeff was released and could breathe again.

Goeff was nine years old, but not too long after that, someone discovered him with an umbrella about to parachute off the garage roof. I guess the daredevil didn't learn anything after the rescue in the basement. I am also guessing he had another eight lives.

Then there was the time he promoted an activity that consisted of challenging the boys in the neighborhood to fight his younger sister, goading them to prove they were tougher than me (younger sister). Of course, I was a tough-and-strong six-year-old fighting machine trained and coached by mister fearless himself; so it was no surprise that I beat up a few boys, and then they stopped coming to fight me.

In the mix of Goeff's experiences, he became a choir boy. This was not unusual for Catholic parishes of the day to have a choir of young boys, many of whom had angelic soprano voices—he was one of those. I think these choirs still exist in some places.

All the while, his place in the family grew in some ways worrisome. He was *moody*, by any definition, and was completely misunderstood by our parents.

It was observed that many an episode of behind-the-door sessions took place between Mama and Goeff, which seemed serious and frequent in these mid years and continued into high school. While we will never know what took place exactly during those heavy and sometimes lengthy meetings—usually in his room—after Mama's death, Goeff told of a disturbing side of his relationship to Mama.

According to Goeff, Mama spent those many hours with him alone in his room incessantly discussing his emerging adolescent sexuality.

The way Goeff explained to me was she was obsessive about it. The way it seemed to him was she set him up for severe guilt related to any sexual feelings.

The family was smitten with Notre Dame football since long ago. The football team was definitely Catholic America's team. I will never know if any other than Catholics were so smitten. This all seemed to culminate in an obsessive desire to attend Notre Dame University on the part of Goeff.

Supported by our parents, this desire grew into a major goal and, if you will, a dream. Lived in imagination, it took hold, and with very little to credit, it became believable. Nothing wrong with dreams and goals, of course, but the sense here is that nothing practical was or even could be done to reach fulfillment. There was nothing to suggest that making this happen was more about dreaming than working to have it happen.

Another place that Goeff seemed to be doomed to failure was his height. At some point, he was notably shorter than he wanted to be in spite of being a high school basketball player. At least in his mind, he did not measure up. So there were novenas and petitions and prayers storming heaven from Goeff, and possibly Mama and Papa as well.

When did he realize that he was never going to be a tall man and with what bitter disappointment? No telling. Perhaps there was resignation, but I have no way to know what happened inside Goeff's self-image. Just know his great hopes and dreams were not to be.

At some point, Goeff went off to slay other dragons.

He reached his teen years and faded from my life, or so it seemed. High school, girls, basketball, and most of all, swimming were preeminent. There came a time when he, like Rose before him, spent weeks in the summertime at either Grandpa's summer home on Lake Erie or Uncle Leo's cottage also on Lake Erie.

While these Lake Erie addresses were many miles apart, they afforded Goeff access to the water, where he learned to distance swim—with the emphasis on *distance*. It was a sight that became legendary as Goeff would dive into the water at Rye Beach or Conneaut and begin his beautifully executed lazy Australian crawl due north. And as he became a smaller and smaller figure in the vast waters, people onshore would call to others near them, "Look at that swimmer! Wow, how far do you think he is out there? Where did he come from?"

And for however long it captured them, they would watch sometimes until Goeff became a mere dot on the horizon. And sometimes disappearing from the sight of the watchers on the shore. He would eventually turn east. He was truly keeping the legacy alive. Rose had done the same thing.

He told of a time when he reached the light house at the very end of a long jetty. When he arrived and began to rest suddenly a large flock of sea gulls began to harass him. After fighting them off for what seemed like hours, he managed to begin his return swim in relative safety. No doubt a little wiser for the experience.

He and Rose both swam without an attending boat. For many reasons, including Lake Erie could become very treacherous very quickly, they were advised to have a boat with at least one person onboard to accompany them. But they never did; they just continued to swim long distances alone.

While he was adventurous and accomplished in many ways, he was an introvert in a family of Irishmen that didn't have much understanding for quiet people. Some would describe him as moody or depressed, others might see some of his reactions more normal for the temperament with which he came. However, that did not explain his rather controlling and sometimes hurtful behavior, especially toward his siblings. My guess is that many families have powerful people disguised as brothers and sisters who, for whatever reason, tend to rule over those they are closest to.

When it came time for him to move on to college, my mother had some of her big plans in the offing. This time, a small elite private Catholic college was her target. With her usual persuasive charm, she began a campaign to get Goeff admitted to this school. My mother never appeared aggressive, but there was a quiet determination that belied her gentle approach, her reserved appearance. It helped that she was very pretty and seemed to have a perfect blend of graciousness and downright flirtatious behavior. Of course, always appearing very proper.

After consulting with various authorities at this great little college, she did it again. This time, Goeff was admitted with some stipulations regarding his viability going forward. In other words, he was very much on probation.

Sure, he tried, but he also was finding more girl friends and a new challenge. He began taking flying lessons and, up to a point, loved it. He got his license and, after having made a hard landing, never flew a plane again. Don't know if it was fear or embarrassment or both.

Goeff was a very good-looking young man. Some of my high school friends dated him, and some of them really fell hard for him. Not certain how good he was at relationships. But suffice it to say once again the ones Mama liked didn't seem to hold his attention for long. In retrospect, it would seem either he was uncomfortable with women who were on equal footing with him, socially and intellectually, or he avoided deepening relationships. The result: his choices cost him dearly.

As with Rose, the recurring theme was no one is going to measure up to our parents' expectations. In Goeff's case, he really tasted of the forbidden fruit. She was pregnant, and he believed the child was his. She was from the other side of the tracks, and she was Slovakian (definitely not among the parental acceptance criteria). Once again, the home at 1211 became a battleground.

Using all the ammo in the arsenal, our parents launched attack after attack resulting in what seemed like a cease fire if not an outright victory. Goeff agreed to stop seeing her; the damage had been done—he flunked out of college, was drafted, and subsequently eloped with the mother of his child. Our parents thought Gene was flawed; nothing compared to Ann in their estimation.

Goeff, his bride—Ann—and newborn George Michael were sent to Texas where Goeff was assigned as a member of the United States Army. There was an elopement, birth of a baby, and deployment of a soldier all within this family but none attended by any family members—quite frankly, little noted or acknowledged. By this time in our history, anger and sorrow were showing signs—or were they harbingers?

Edward (My Brother)

E dward James, the fourth child of Cal and Marie, entered the world in January 1940. The youngest in a family of four children, there are a lot of things good about that, and some not so good. So let's see how Edward fared.

To start with, he was an adorable baby. Maybe some prejudice here, but I can tell you this: his arrival conjured serious feelings of jealousy. It was clear he was the center of it all now in that January 1940, and I had no idea how to handle these dark feelings.

There came a time, which did not take too long, where I made up my mind to quit the bad stuff (not liking that baby boy because he usurped my place) and put something else in place of it. You would think it was sheer will, a decision to change my attitude. Maybe so, but nothing could have prepared me for what happened and kept happening the rest of my life. I loved Edward as if he was my child. In my eyes, there was never a more beautiful child. And truth be known, he was a sweetheart inside and out.

I doted over him, took care of him, and did for him in one amazing display of love; and it was deep. Nothing ever came between us.

When we were old enough to relate as children, we began a journey. It included pure delight in going to movies together. We would see some repeatedly, up to fourteen times, until we knew the dialogue and would begin play sessions in which each would reenact a part in the movie. I was the lead, and Ed often took the role of sidekick. Most of the time they were supportive but occasionally adversarial. Those I can remember clearly to this day.

Somewhere in our memory bank are scenes with dialogue of *Wild Harvest*. Alan Ladd was the star, and Robert Preston supporting. A tale about harvest time on the *Great Plains*. And then there was *The Three Musketeers*. Oh my, that was ambitious. Between the bedrooms and hall at 1211, many imaginary foes were overcome—and, truly, they weren't so imaginary because we memorized the plot, the characters, and the dialogue which lent a reality outside of imagination.

We lived that and believed it had importance in each of our lives.

Then there was the season which went on and on in which I took my brother everywhere I went and insisted he be included. For the most part, it worked. My friends who wanted to be with us or go with us would give in to the rule that Ed was going too. If that was not agreeable, they knew they weren't welcome. Probably thinned out a few friends, but mostly the real ones stayed in.

Edward was always kind and sensitive, and still is. Family gatherings of the daily kind, i.e. dinner. We would all (parents and siblings) be at the table, each with their stories of the day, and mostly Papa telling of conquering the lions at the mill. He told many tales of conflict and frustration peppered with his manly language. When he cursed about something or someone, Mama would always admonish with this phrase, "Oh, Cal!" which translated: *Do you really need to use that language in front of your family?*

One constant at these wonderful mealtimes was Edward watching and listening as each of us would expound our tales of the day. He was the quiet observer, nary a trace of judgment or criticism. On the contrary, he left the impression he was interested in what each of us had to say.

Then the summer of his twelfth year came. It was a life changer: he became ill. I remember the phone calls, this one between my mama and me in which she told me Ed was hospitalized. (I was vacationing with a friend on Long Island, and Ed was with Mama at Rye Beach.)

Once again, the family was experiencing a chaotic and frightening time. Ed was eventually diagnosed with juvenile diabetes. A very consuming disease. You lose your freedom with this disease. Until you can learn about it and how your body works, it is a dire struggle, and I watched as it all but consumed Ed and Mama and, to come extent, Papa.

The terror of watching your son in insulin shock and learning you are the first line of defense and what to do to literally save him until the ambulance could get there was part of the new normal at our house. Many the time, I watched my mama and Papa coaxing orange juice and sugar through Ed's clenched jaws as he lay on the floor sometimes slightly spastic and sometimes rigid. If there was just an opening enough to get it into his mouth—all the while believing if you failed, he could be lost. Often after such an episode, he would spend days in the hospital while they regulated what was an out-of-control insulin/glucose system in his body.

Frequent doctors visits were laced with doctor acknowledgment that Ed would be lucky to see twenty-five or, at the most, thirty years of age. His was an extreme case.

All the while the tenure and tone of the household was as serious and somber as much about doing what needed to be done for Ed as anything else that was going on, and there were developments lurking.

In some ways, the preoccupation Mama had with thinking and fussing and worrying and cooking and staying alert to his needs may have actually been helpful in a weird way with some of the upcoming family circumstances.

But at the time, it was a learning curve—what you do in the event of insulin shock which needs to be very quick. And on the other hand, how do you know when the victim is heading for a coma brought on by severely high blood sugar? Mama never really slept soundly after Ed was diagnosed; she lived in the fear he would shock during the night in his sleep. It did happen, and that ended any hope of having a deep and restful sleep for Mama.

In those days, they used strips dipped in the patient's urine to determine their glucose levels, accompanied by finger sticks and blood readings. And then, of course, there were the injections, most of the time multiple shots in one day. This seemed never to get better; Ed always had to inject himself several times in a twenty-four-hour period.

There was always much consideration and sometimes consternation about diet, a very important component to the care and treatment of diabetes. Mama learned everything she possibly could about what was good and safe and what was forbidden or unsafe. It was more complicated than simply eliminating sugar.

Frankly, that was bad enough. She would often prepare Ed's individual meal and another one for the rest of us. Ahead of her time, she became conscious of the importance of a healthy diet. Also, she was aware of and was encouraging Ed to exercise. This was 1952, a very long time before the exercise and diet craze became the rule of the day.

Ed took a course based on Charles Atlas. Using body-building techniques proved very helpful in literally shaping Ed's life and body. As the ads stated, he went from a ninety-pound weakling to an astonishing 175 pounds in a matter of weeks. He was dedicated and disciplined. Not long after he met his goal, he trained me to lift weights and eat small meals five times a day. He also introduced me to the milkshake with an egg in it as an everyday regime. I had been ill, and my five-foot, eight-inch frame was emaciated with only ninety-eight pounds on it. When I left the program he established, I weighed 122 and was gaining.

It was sometime after that Ed began to train as a boxer. Two things occurred: he won his first fight, and Mama and I could hardly stand it waiting at home to learn the outcome. Truly it is hard to imagine what fighter families go through.

Until someone disclosed that Ed was diabetic, he continued in training for the Golden Gloves. In the meantime, he kept his fighting activity from the family, shielding us from the emotional toll. We knew he was training but did not realize he had sixteen fights and won all but two of them. Well on his way, you might say, until the bad news came. The gym manager informed him he could no longer train there, giving some vague excuse that "we have to let you go because we are overextended" (a paraphrase).

This was not the last time this disease stopped him. He was signed up to take flying lessons when he learned that avenue was also closed.

Ed kept going and, in the midst, joined me in an effort to start a modeling school in a nearby southeastern Ohio town. With minimal funding, we began related research. This took us to NYC and a venture that became an adventure.

We were welcomed into the world of high-fashion modeling of that day, including a luncheon with Candy Jones, the Cindy Crawford of the 1950s. We met at Roosevelt Bar in midtown Manhattan during Fashion Week and discussed the modeling school business. We also visited John Robert Powers for an interview regarding starting a school in Ohio.

But the most outstanding evidence we were being taken seriously was the interview at Barbizon. We were escorted to a backroom at the downtown Manhattan modeling school. All employees who were present treated us with respect, but a whiff of paranoia seemed to permeate and we were subject to questions regarding our intentions. It had the feel of an interrogation, not a sharing of advice as the others had been. Could it be that they thought we were scoping and snooping in order to launch some kind of direct competition?

In fact, one of the chief players at that meeting—who appeared to be an executive—clearly stated that competition in this field was discouraged.

We came home from our NYC experience; found a perfect rental to begin our business; and from there, everything faded away. Perhaps reality set in when we looked at our funds versus what we would have to spend, or maybe it was just old-fashioned cold feet. The sad thing is we will never know what our dream/plans could have meant to the area, and honestly, we had some really good ideas. The appetite for modeling training was growing at that time, and the mid-sized city we picked had enough sophistication to support this kind of business to the point of flourishing. It was a good dream.

Somewhere along the way, I bought a sports car. Ed and I went through a wonderful season enjoying the car, cleaning the car, polishing the car, painting the wire wheels on the car, buying aesthetic additions for the car, having the car repaired, and finally driving the car on the back roads of western Pennsylvania. It was glorious.

There came a time when Ed would drop me off at work and he would take the car to school and whatever. I trusted my brother completely, but neither of us were prepared for the accident: Ed was suffering a low sugar emergency and asked his friend to drive him home. Unfortunately, his friend did not drive. He made it all the way home and smashed into another car when he pulled up to park in front of 1211.

The good news is no one was hurt, and Ed got the care he needed. The bad news is because the marketplace was skewed, the car sat for months waiting for important parts. It did not help that the body-man recommended to me was most likely a functioning alcoholic and, frankly, was not functioning all that well.

To this day, I think the guilt my brother carried—and to some extent, still does—could have altered our relationship, but we just wouldn't let it.

This, too, did pass, and Ed went for a wonderful ride into his late teens and early twenties. During this time, he began to take guitar lessons at a music school in Pittsburgh. When he had mastered the instrument to the standard of his instructors, they hired him to teach, and he was launched into a music career for a few very happy years. Something he could do, he did well and was not forbidden by the disease.

He became a professional entertainer when a group formed to play the music of the day, which was mostly rock and roll. The group played many clubs in the area and were kept busy even as openers for some noted performers of that day. After two-and-a-half years, their drummer went to Las Vegas, they morphed to jazz and blues, and eventually found other avenues to travel individually.

This was a closed chapter that led to an opened door. Radio was Ed's latest conquest, and it worked *marvelously*. He worked at a radio station in Weirton, West Virginia. He was the morning DJ and was a perfect fit. The listeners appreciated his down-to-earth almost down-home way of talking to them every day in between spinning the record hits of the day. He knew and loved music and could connect with his audience as only an Irishman with a godlike voice and a story telling gift, not to mention the inimitable sense of humor. He was in the styles, combining Arthur Godfrey and Steve Allen. The people loved him, and to a large extent, he returned the affection.

I don't know if he would ever have left, except the family moved to Ohio. In Northern Ohio, he found another niche—a country western station in Erie, Pennsylvania. Different music, different audience, different state, but the same success—the listeners tuned in to hear this man with *the voice* who could connect with them just as he had in West Virginia.

Ed had surely found a great place for himself. He was good at it, and it seemed this perfect situation would just keep on going.

This time, the family move would change everything. Ed decided to venture out to California where they, the family, were congregating to join his brother Goeff, who preceded them to the Golden State. This time, things were different. All Ed's skills, experience, and natural affinity for radio were not enough; the market in Northern California was, in reality, closed. No room for new personalities. He had come back from many disappointments. None quite like this.

In order to take care of himself in this almost-hostile territory, he began a job hunt that led him to an employment agency. He was trying to find a new niche. Instead he found the love of his life and, ultimately, his bride and very faithful wife—who have been together for over forty years as of this writing.

In the meantime, he chauffeured, drove a cab, and generally faced life with a dogged determination that kept him going forward. He would probably say sideways. Later he would become a valued employee with a security company working as a guard.

And Me—Your Witness

I n the fall of my nineteenth year, my mother and I agreed I would
go to help Goeff and Ann—now husband and wife—with their
newborn baby boy. Goeff was stationed in Fort Worth, Texas,
with the army. They lived on Lake Worth in a tiny, tiny cottage.

As helper in residence, I helped Ann—mother of George
Michael—with many chores, but the one that best illustrates the lifestyle was washing by hand the many cloth diapers needed for this
newborn. One step in the process of cleaning these was boiling them
on the stove, and the other was washing by hand. That memory is
so stark that I have no recall of how we hung those dozens of diapers
to dry.

All went well albeit labor intensive. Ann seemed to welcome
the help, and we got along just fine. On the other hand, my brother
Goeff was withdrawn to the point of depression. He was functioning
but from a very dark place that Ann and I could only puzzle about
but had no way to intervene and had no understanding for what had
happened to take him away from us.

I lasted a couple of weeks and was home, filling the family in
on all that I had witnessed by the first week in October. Now I can't
remember if I told how Goeff had withdrawn in a profound way. It
really doesn't matter, because nothing could have prepared us for the
phone calls we were about to receive on October 11 and 13.

First the call letting us know the infant son of Goeff and Ann had died. Two days later, the unimaginable call reporting Goeff—the father of infant George Michael—was arrested for the murder of his seven-week-old son.

This is Goeff—our son; our brother. There is some mistake, of course, this is not really happening. I can't get up from the floor where I landed upon hearing this; some unseen force is kicking me in the stomach repeatedly.

Much of the next week remains a blur of the family making decisions about who and when each would go. Gene—Rose's husband—devoted himself to all of us and actually went with our Papa to Fort Worth to help in whatever way was needed.

With little fanfare and some measure of personal sacrifice, Gene came alongside the people that had trouble accepting him into the family originally. A gesture not lost on any of us, most especially Mama and Papa. Actually, it was more than a gesture—much more. He was a presence for Papa in many ways as they attempted to learn and access what to do in the days following Goeff's arrest.

Aside from absorbing the shock of it all, they had to find out what needed to be done to help Goeff, his case, and his cause. Navigating the legal waters for people who found themselves in new waters. No one can know what it is like on the other side of the law until it happens to you. It seems as if you have entered another world, and for one thing, it doesn't seem safe—as if there is really no one there for you.

Dark waters that are darker still because nothing seems the same as it had always been. You left the world of light and comfort and familiarity, and the door closed behind you.

You needed to learn how to act and interact. What your role was—what you could and could not do. Where you were allowed and where it was forbidden. The father's role was to find an attorney for your accused son. Before that, find out just what the DA was saying; and before that, what your son was saying all while trying to comfort your son and yourself. By far the hardest thing for our father.

Then there's the media when you are greeted by a frontpage picture of your son's hands titled, *Are these the hands of a murderer?*

It gives you pause or stabs your heart. When every evening newscast features the horrific crime your son is accused of, and to which he has confessed. These nightly broadcasts were in Fort Worth, Texas, and in Pittsburgh and went on for what seemed like weeks. Night after night, talk about being on the other (wrong) side of the law and what that feels like, being on the other side of the media is equally painful and frightening. This was 1954; I can't imagine what it would be like today.

Then very bizarre happenings, such as the neighbor in our hometown Pennsylvania, calling the police to inform them that there was a dead baby in our house on Boundary St. hundreds of miles from where the actual crime took place. Who thought that it happened at our house? A whiff of darkness about the Boundary St. house proved to be a harbinger of future revelations.

The intrusion of reporters, so-called, doing their job. They called our house and hounded my father and his son-in-law, Gene. Subsequently, they called hotels where they knew family members were staying. In some ways, you sort of go away in your mind to escape this onslaught. You try to deal with the reality on at least two levels: find a way to accept that this actually happened, and to find a way to be in the world with that fact. All the while staying standing. That didn't always happen.

Then there were attorneys to choose and decisions to make on a daily basis. Everything from who to trust to counsel and consent about how to defend. These were made in secret, and much of the decision-making details remain secret to this day.

Another side to the story, and there are several, deals with the people of the city of Fort Worth. Most of the public opinion did not like my brother and found no excuse for understanding for him. My mother seemed to be an innocent victim of that judgment. When she went to a salon to ensure she kept up her appearance, the beautician consoled her in a deep and surprising way. She likened my mother's grief for her son to the grief of Mary, the mother of Jesus. This was one of the many such interactions with a different and empathetic side of Fort Worth.

And still, another side, Ann—Goeff's wife—engaged in some questionable decision-making of her own. She, dare I say, *sold* the story to a *True Crime Magazine*. Needless to say, this did nothing to help the relationship with my family.

While all this was going on, one constant was Gene—my brother-in-law—who was not only by my father's and, ultimately, mother's side but offered immeasurable support on the emotional level as well as the legal and decision-making side. Gene had studied to be an attorney and knew a bit about the law and the way things worked. He could not only help navigate these waters but, in a wonderfully loving and practical way, steer the ship. He was invaluable.

Then came January 1955, and the trial began. It was difficult at best and excruciating at worst. The plea was not guilty by reason of insanity. And the defense that both my family and the attorneys set about trying to prove was that Goeff was insane, schizophrenic to be exact. In order to present that defense, you were forced to view him through the lens of strange behavior and report to the court every behavior of the defendant that could be understood as mental illness. You would not wish this on anyone. Your life laid opened and scrutinized to be judged insane. On the other side, the state was asking for the death penalty.

The days of the trial are hard to recall. I can report that psychiatrists ruled the day. One saying Goeff was insane, and another saying he was seriously maladjusted but not insane. A dramatic moment came when the psychiatrist who had testified for the defense was called out. A witness took the stand and was asked what title this doctor had in the community, and the answer was Dr. Schizophrenia. Turns out he had appeared in many court cases in that jurisdiction proclaiming the defendant (he was a witness for the defense in every case) was indeed suffering from schizophrenia. Needless to say, this was not a good day for the defense. However, in retrospect, this may have been a good day for Goeff.

After my mother testified and Goeff's wife testified, neither of which I have any recall, there were a few others who came to support the insanity plea and then the defense rested.

I will tell you the news reports of these testimonies are hard to read since the premise was flawed and caused people to insinuate or outright state that this person on trial for his life is and was, due to insanity, unable to know what he was doing at the time he committed these acts.

He confessed to squeezing his baby to death. He had engaged in this several times over a period of days. As with all such inexplicable acts, no matter how much you tell details or try to find motive, nothing satisfies the desire to understand. Some interesting facts are: Goeff agreed to an autopsy upon which the detectives based the confession, which Goeff agreed to sign.

When you reflect on the guilty verdict, you come to the realization that if we had won the case, Goeff's fate would have been seriously compromised since the result would have been incarceration in a mental hospital for the criminally insane. However, when you are fighting to avoid death in the electric chair, your reasoning and the conclusion can be desperate. I am not privy to the decision-making.

On January 15, 1955, Goeff was found guilty of murdering his seven-week-old baby boy and was sentenced to ninety-nine years in prison, ending the horrific journey that began in that tiny cottage on Lake Worth on or about October 1, 1954, when this young man had admittedly squeezed the life out of his infant son.

As you would expect, those who were in the courtroom—members of his family, including his wife, mother of the slain baby boy—were inconsolable. Although Papa managed to talk to his son on the one hand, trying to buoy him, while his brother Ed went into shock in his attempt to cope. I became hysterical, and my mama held Goeff and just cried. Ann hugged, kissed, and held her husband in her arms.

The following day, he was transported to Huntsville Prison (notably a tough place), and the families—Goeff's and Ann's— returned to their respective homes, never to connect again (with one curious exception much later).

When we began to deal with the reality, it was game on Texas.

Not in anger or bitterness but in the heart attitude, we were about to launch a campaign to get our brother—our son—out of Texas, whatever it took. One of those no-stone unturned situations.

Needless to say, we had to learn who, how and when to do this but do it we would for the ensuing years.

Many people joined us in writing letters to anyone they were told was significant. Contacts and behind-the-scenes endeavors went on for months and years.

We would learn later, much later, the most important matter was how Goeff fared in that environment. On the one hand, we were not surprised to discover he was doing quite well. We were delighted to find he was involved in helping many, in instituting many thoughtful ways to make things better for the prisoners, and in giving very practical assistance to them. He helped by typing letters for fellow inmates when they needed to communicate with lawyers and officials regarding many matters.

In the in-house publication, there was an article entitled "Let Goeff Do It." It featured my brother in all the various endeavors, activities, and undertakings. He installed piped-in classical music in the dinning room. He was an avid chess player and had a group in the prison who joined him. He played trumpet in the band. This band played at the rodeos during the season. He was one of the inmates who visited high schools to encourage teens to live good lives and think twice about their choices.

He also had a job, at one time, in the library. And he became the projectionist in charge of the movies that were shown to the prisoners.

And then a newspaper article dated August 16, 1964 stated: "The people who came to know Goeff when he entered the state penitentiary at Huntsville could only say he made a model prisoner."

He worked as a bookkeeper in the commissary. He was bright and very quiet, in the opinion of the prison officials. Goeff, at twenty-two, was sent to Huntsville for a ninety-nine-year sentence. It was a terrific blow to his parents and his young wife. What it was to Goeff, he would never say.

I asked him at the time if he thought he would ever tend to commit such violence again.

He answered, "No, never."

I asked him how he knew he wouldn't.

"I just know," he said. "I just know."

That was nine-and-a-half years ago.

On July 7, 1964, Goeff was paroled.

He went to California to begin all over again.

I wished him luck. He seemed to be a nice, quiet young man.

In another interview, it is reported one prison official is quoted, "I would like to have one prisoner come in like him. I don't want him back. I want him to make good. He worked just like an employee." He continued, "He's got a wonderful brain."

Another said, "Everything just rolled smooth for him." He never broke prison rules, according to information in his record in the warden's office.

And in the prison's point incentive program, his mark was 160—called very high by one prison employee. He was released July 7; this was 1964.

I've recorded some of the ways people, as well as Goeff, spoke about him during the Fort Worth experience:

> "...he is not overly nervous. He's polite,
> soft-spoken. He appears just a normal guy. Not
> too loud, not too retiring."

His wife said, "Goeff loved the baby. He would play with it and love it and talk of what he would be when he grew up."

One examining psychiatrist commented, "A very definite emotional conflict is usually found in cases like this. Goeff said he believes he has some sort of maladjustment. What else," he asked "could account for the thing he did?"

He wondered why he would do it and even prayed that he would stop.

"I loved the baby. My wife and I wanted the baby. There must be some reason for what I did." Goeff was quoted as saying.

During an interview, Goeff shook his head and said, "I am as much at a loss in trying to explain the murder as you are," he told a reporter.

He was also quoted as saying, "There must be a reason for what I did, but I just can't find it. I didn't intend to kill the baby."

It was recorded that Goeff asked for the autopsy or, at the very least, agreed to it. "I knew I would not get away with it. I knew I would have it on my conscience the rest of my life."

When he talked to reporters after he was arrested, he was coherent and polite but said he was confused about why he had crushed the baby. He described it as a spontaneous instinct.

A reporter described him in the courtroom during the trial as emotionless, looking pale, and wearing a slight frown.

His wife said his mental condition caused him to destroy the child.

Another thing to tell here is the response on the part of some members of the Fort Worth community. Those that made phone calls to the family to offer sympathy and condolences when they learned of the verdict. I can assure you this was very comforting. And it says something about that community.

The actual parole date was July 7, 1964.

The first correspondence from Goeff following his release is a postcard depicting Elm St., Dallas. The site of Kennedy's assassination, which he visited and later wrote about to his family. This was his first stop on the trip to San Francisco, where his new life was waiting for him.

A boyhood friend, who was our neighbor on Boundary St. and who was now a Christian Pastor in Northern California, was his sponsor. He was instrumental in helping Goeff with all his needs in this part of his journey. This family will be forever grateful to this man.

The story of his adjustment and the choices he made from this new starting point in his life are at least another chapter in this family's history.

Suffice it to say, he was free, and his attitude reflected his appreciation of that alone.

And There Was Joshua

His name was Joshua; I'd known him for two years. Two years of occasional visits from him, usually at my place of work. Also, I would see him at the sports car club meetings because we both belonged to the local club. He was a nice, regular guy. A little quiet but seemed interested in my life, although I never quite knew why.

Then one day I found myself seated in a room full of men (male scuba divers), and he was there; and somehow, for the very first time, I *saw* how handsome he was. I was at the meeting because he had invited me, which thrilled me.

It all started happening one night when he and his friend Mike met me in the middle of the street. I was riding around town, looking for my *real* love when these two stopped their car and, after some snappy talk, invited me to join them at a club. We sat at the bar and laughed our way through two or three hours.

At the end of the evening, I'd arranged for Mike to teach me to scuba dive. I had decided I was through with sports car racing.

The day for the first lesson arrived, and Mike sent Josh in his place (de Bergerac-like). He was still the nice, regular guy, but I was learning that Josh was far more interesting than I had suspected. In fact, he was absolutely intriguing.

Gently he led me through instruction and demonstration and encouraged me to try each technique without any sense of superiority or macho in spite of the fact he was a practiced and experienced scuba diver. I can't recall what I learned, only that I was never made to feel stupid or inept thanks to Josh.

Meanwhile, this kind, patient, gentle person provoked me with his questions. "Why do you smoke?" No one had ever asked me, so why did he want to know? He would ask, then watch and listen intently while I probed my inner awareness for the truth. Much more an observer as the inquisitor he was fascinating.

Unlike anyone I had ever known, he was not predictable; on the contrary, he was unique beyond description. There was always a sense of genuine interest as if he really considered me important enough to want to know about everything that concerned me. What I misunderstood, at least at first, was his heart toward me. I discerned that his heart toward others was empathetic.

One of the first evenings we spent together—following one of the lessons—we stopped at a drive-in restaurant (the rage at that time), and for several hours, we discussed feelings and what was important and significant. Let me tell you this was unlike any conversation I'd ever had with a man.

I hesitate to write the dialog because it would be so easy to lose the sense of what I learned that evening. I am careful not to make common what he said to me in the telling of it. So it is difficult. Usually dialog can help to describe and circumscribe; not so here.

Josh had a purity and innocence inside a soul that defied plumbing for; alongside, there was a sorrow—a piercing so deep I struggled to hold back the tears as I listened to him, sitting in the car in the back row of the drive-in restaurant. What I didn't know then: I was beginning to *love* this man.

Also what I didn't know then was the other side of Josh. It didn't really matter. By the time he gave a few scuba lessons and we had dinner together at a little Italian restaurant where he asked me more about me—and of course the drive-in time together—it wasn't long before sitting across the room from this man I could truly say I was getting to know him, he was letting me know him, and that he's one handsome dude. Funny, I had never noticed, during all those visits in the previous two years, how handsome he was.

I don't remember how it evolved, but there came a time following that meeting in the room full of scuba divers that Josh and I talked every day, commuting to work (for me) and school (for him) together. We both went to Pittsburgh, and it became part of the wonder and life we had together to either drive there or ride the bus together every day. Again it was unlike any romance, any relationship, I'd ever known.

If I'd ever been in love before, it had never been anything like this—not even close. We would spend lunch hour(s) in his VW bug, overlooking the river from various vantage points in the city. We had our brown bags, and he'd buy the beverages in the train station nearby. So many delightful little rituals—like buying roasted peanuts and bags of cherries from the street vendors and finding wonderful places in parks throughout the city to sit and lie; catching the bus and sitting on the very back seat in the stickiest heat, crowded in on all sides; and feeling happy and having fun, so much fun.

These days were truly the most fun days of my life, and he was a wonder man in every important way. How could I not be in love?

I wish I could describe the scuba-club meetings we went to. Josh's humor was more than joking or clowning, although there was definitely both of those; it was a perspective uniquely his. A wit, dry and creative and very natural—it was more a part of how he thought. Another facet of Josh? He is, in a sense, a humorist.

The beauty of what happened that summer so long ago was unlike anyone before or since. He made me come alive in remarkable ways. I felt freer, finer, smarter, and funnier because this man thought I was all of those things. Because he made me feel as if he believed all those things about me, they came true in my life during that glorious summer.

We laughed and played our way through those scuba meetings as if we were observing the others from somewhere many of them could not be. It was so fun, but there were other aspects I'll tell later. There's a lot to tell later.

Often we would meet for breakfast in the city—crowded places, busy and hurried—but it felt so good to be with him. He challenged me in many ways, but he never overwhelmed me. Although there were places I perhaps should have seen as potentially overwhelming. But now, in the summer that year, we had so much to say, to share, to laugh at; and then he would ask me to read a book. Somerset Maugham's *Of Human Bondage* was the first one. I loved it and thought perhaps he was trying to tell me something with the story of Maugham's lead character.

This brings me to another important part of what was happening in all this summertime happiness. The underlying theme for me: I was your typical scarlet woman, reputation and all. I clearly remember Josh's brother, Matt, musing that he couldn't understand how Josh could become involved with a woman like me. After all, wasn't Josh the quiet, straight, clean-living young student, unspoiled, unsophisticated by the standards of that day? The message was clearly delivered, ironically, to the daughter of class and ethnic snobs.

I'd become accustomed to all sorts of men; remember, this was in the 1950s. Sexuality was basically a hush-hush subject, a hidden matter. To be promiscuous in those days would seem rather tame by comparison to today's activities. I've always considered myself a forerunner of the sexual revolution. That way, it sounds socially and historically acceptable. It was anything but that in my mind and conscience.

I felt I was lowly, ugly, shameful, disgusting—you name it; I truly hated what I'd become during my twenties. Once, I came clean with Josh, confessing my lifestyle. Incredibly he accepted me as if he didn't need to accept me. As if he didn't see me as needing to *be accepted*. Much more, he just couldn't help himself. To him I was worth loving—lovable, if you will. Without question, it was as if this man *saved* me from myself and a lifestyle in which I had become entrapped and felt helpless to change.

Mixed in with all this was a puzzling and different stance of Josh. Unlike nearly every man I had ever known, Josh did not attempt to become physical with me early in the summertime. While I consider those days ever so romantic, there was little—if any—touching.

I couldn't bring myself to talk about his backwardness; I was curious and relieved at the same time. It was nice not to have all that heavy stuff clouding nearly everything else. What I didn't realize at this time was my sexual dysfunction was fairly extreme, and it had little to do with the time I was living in.

In the book *Of Human Bondage*, the main character was in love with a prostitute. I guess I was afraid to discuss this with Josh; as I think of it now, I know the fear lay in two places. It was risky to broach the issue of the similarities between myself and the prostitute and far too scary to analyze the male character's motivation and limitation. Also, I kept my secret place from Josh. I never thought I was intelligent enough for him. I believed somehow I was pulling it off. Perhaps so many things were right between us that it may not ever matter, and I didn't care as long as our relationship kept working so, so well.

I wondered if the message of the book from Josh to me was the tremendous discrepancy between the two main characters. He was brilliant and sensitive and had a club foot. She was cheap; trashy; shallow; rather stupid; street-smart, maybe, but barely even that; narcissistic; and emotionally void. He was totally unable to help himself; she had captivated him and held him as if he had no will beyond wanting her until she completely crushed any feeling he had.

My worries were 1) Josh was hiding the fact that he was handicapped. Unlike the book hero, Josh's was in a manner not evident, I imagined, as the character's club foot; 2) Josh was more captivated, obsessed with me than anything good or committed; and 3) most importantly, that I would ultimately be a disappointment to him, which is something I've always believed.

To clarify, I never let myself dwell on the negatives of all this. Everything was far too positive in our relationship; it was easy to let those worries slide into the background and enjoy what was happening.

Another place I refused to go were the evidences of a dark side. When you've met your perceived savior, you begin to believe in magic as perhaps never before in your life. This was certainly true for me.

Manifested in this remarkable man was a dark, mysterious person capable of shutting everyone out to the point of cruelty. Withdrawing behind a wall so impenetrable you were totally cut off from him. I learned to adjust to the silence and a sense of rage and rejection. This was all he left behind when he withdrew. Often I had no idea what I'd done or said to cause him to leave. Now I know it wasn't always me. Although I was left, abandoned.

We married December 2, 1961, and, for the next seven and a half years, went about having babies: Amy, Craig, and Eric. And without any help from our friends, we attempted to be a family.

Josh was a political reporter for a newspaper in a town nearby. I managed to stay at home for obvious reasons. We lived in a cozy little house in a resort village on Lake Erie in Northern Ohio. It all sounds idyllic; there was a Beatles song about this perfectly amazing young woman who got married and became very bland. I could have written those lyrics. What I feared did indeed come upon me. Not particularly good at being a wife, and equally questionable at parenting, no one but the family could know.

On the other hand, sharing some darkness, Josh and I simply kept it going until it got off track and eventually ended. The darkness thing was hidden deep inside family history. The marriage had, as all do, many twists and turns; but shortly after purchasing our dream house, the dream became a personal nightmare culminating in Josh, finding someone to go away with.

The part of me I gave to him, he trampled. The part of him he gave to me was beyond my comprehension. The failure was mutual. He abandoned us.

Me Again but I Don't Know How to Do This

Grieving and mourning deep loss while facing your young children every day was most difficult. In my feeble attempt to comfort the children (Eric, the youngest was six months old), I explained that their dad was unhappy and went away to spare us his unhappiness. There was truth in that. Amy was six, and Craig was four.

Now let me take some time to tell you a little about these children God gave us. Amy, the firstborn, possessed a wisdom beyond her years, and the role she took in the family when Josh left was coming alongside me.

Craig was a happy-and-energetic child who would spend most of his life trying to overcome the deficit of a missing father. He was, for me, challenging and rewarding. As he grew, he took on a protective/provider role. To illustrate this child's awareness at age four, he was heard to say, "We are all weird in our own way" while observing adults behaving strangely.

And then there's Eric. He never really knew his dad except as a returning one when Josh would come to visit. Temperamentally, only one description fit: wild child. Born into grief and chaos, he reflected some of both those realities. However, what made it even more so was he was bright and—no surprise—he had ADD/ADHD. For me, all this was overwhelming. I wasn't prepared or equipped, but then I don't think anyone is. My experience when this becoming-a-single-parent happened: my life changed in every way.

I would describe it as not ever being able to simply walk again. At least not for the ensuing nineteen years. It was as if I was running, running, running, and was always behind. Never able to catch up and/or catch on. I felt in the dark as far as understanding what the children needed or wanted; I just kept going, headlong and blind. And, of course, never getting enough sleep. On a given Saturday morning, I would be awakened by some crisis or another.

Classic example: I remember well the Saturday the boys were up ahead of me and were undoubtedly trying to make breakfast. There was a lot of noise, clatter, and finally laughter. It could have been worse, but it is just characteristic. Someone—to this day, I am not sure just who was responsible—had spilled or poured or otherwise dispensed the contents of an entire Cheerios box onto the kitchen floor. This is a simple episode, but there were many more serious and sometimes frightening ones.

I want to illustrate another phase of Eric. At the urging of a salesperson, I purchased a toy guaranteed to be unbreakable. You guessed it: he broke it in about fifteen minutes. The guarantee was honored, and I bought another unbreakable toy home to Eric. This time, it didn't take even fifteen minutes. I didn't know whether to be embarrassed, which I was getting used to, or dubious of the claim the toy manufacturer was touting.

This child was not your average two-year-old. They should have hired him to *test* their product. Eric had a slight build: small, red-haired, fair-skinned, but had brown eyes—just what I had ordered. Everyone in my family was blue-eyed—three were redheads, and one was a blond.

Three things occur to me as I write this: I am privileged to have been ignorant of many antics they performed in those days. Eric was always moving and finding things to disturb and destroy, or was doing something that would frighten the beholder. He really never seemed malevolent, always just curious or adventuresome. Never knowing or seeing the danger to himself or others, or perceiving the destruction for what it was. Just crashing through life on a tear and a mission that adults didn't understand.

The last thing to add here is that the behaviors grew in seriousness as the boys grew in age. Meanwhile, Amy's sensibleness kept us all sane, or at least it seemed that way to me. She did seem to enjoy her high school days with friends and a certain kind of frolic and managed to have a fifteen minutes of rebellion as a young adult. Full-throated but managed to keep boundaries. I knew how the children felt about each other—in particular, where Amy was concerned. Once, in a heart-to-heart talk I had with Craig, he stated, "Amy is so good she makes it hard for us" (him and his brother).

Each of my children, in their own way, have blessed me immeasurably. They have varied and interesting pasts, but at this writing, they are very productive people who bring much to my life and the lives of many. I am exceedingly grateful.

As I conclude this part of the family story, let me say this: Amy is a highly successful administrator in a large medical complex in San Francisco, using her skills and education to provide care to mostly older citizens. She definitely has a heart for the elderly among us. I like to say my daughter enjoys helping senior citizens, and I am delighted because I am one of them. She has also been in the performing arts as a dancer and actor and now in her work as an excellent presenter and instructor.

Craig has reinvented himself several times. At age twenty-two, he started his own business. That entrepreneur spirit has served him well as he forged waters of change in business and his career. He has a wonderful mind (echoes of his grandparents), is mathematically endowed, a logical thinker, and is able to persuade others. Contracting in electronics and in construction has also been in his experience.

Eric has strengths in the arts and technology. He has created a portfolio of work ranging from hundreds of automobile designs, as a teenage boy, to computer art and photography. He is one who gets to make a living at something he loves and in which he has talent. Presently working at an advertising agency as production artist.

They all live and work in the Bay Area in California.

Heaven Sent Help

I digressed and want to go back to explaining my life as a single mom.

There was a woman whose name was Vivian who became my friend a year or so before Josh left. The reality is she knew Josh, me, and the children. She also knew a woman named Elle, who had befriended Vivian at a point when Vivian was trying to help Elle learn some different realities—that marriage and family and love really can work.

Elle had become exceedingly cynical. Using us as an illustration, she introduced Elle to our family, believing Elle would see an intact family that exuded all that goodness. Elle did indeed agree; however, when Josh went away, she was the woman who went with him.

Needless to say, Vivian was horrified by this and tried to help me and the children. So she moved into our home after they left. Turns out, she was more than a help: she led me to a place which completely changed my life and still stands as the most important relationship I have ever had.

Vivian was an extraordinary woman. She truly laid down her life for me and, therefore, my children also. Before she moved into my life, my heart, and my home, she and her former husband had owned a furniture store. She had raised three sons and was divorced.

Mary worked in retail sales and was very successful. She was always attuned to the person more than simply treating them as a customer.

Once—months prior to Josh's departure—when she was visiting me in my colonial center hall home, sparsely furnished since Josh and I never had the opportunity to furnish anything but the basics, she looked around at the spacious and relatively empty rooms. She said, "My furniture would look great in your house." Prophetic words that neither of us could have realized at the time.

Not long after Josh left, the day came when Vivian moved in with me and my children. Her fourteen-year-old son came with her. Hank was amazing, quite like his mother.

He was bright and caring and had many years of wisdom ahead of fourteen. He became a delightful big brother to my children and a great friend to me.

Meanwhile, Vivian and I began a journey that not only was life changing for me but was quite interesting for both of us. There was a season when Vivian simply listened to me. We were both working; so in the evenings at the kitchen table, I would pour out the pain of loss and confusion I was feeling all the while trying to understand what had happened and why.

Vivian let me pour out and rarely judged, but she would bring me back gently to reality and caution. I didn't realize at the time, but her aim was to help me through without getting snagged on bitterness or hatred. This experience led to a search we agreed to enter together.

We began to read philosophers and at least one seer. We searched in the works of Kierkegaard and Nietzsche and others—also Edgar Casey. We spent hours sharing our findings, ideas, and interpretations of these men. This went on for many months. I now believe it was helpful in occupying me with something other than me. I know it was the prelude to finding the one-and-only truth for my life.

Vivian's son—Hank—and I enjoyed a relationship of some depth and understanding. So that on a Thursday evening in Holy Week, when he asked what happened on that night, I was excited to tell him all I knew. And I knew a bit since I had been raised in the Catholic Church.

Catholics are very aware of the history of Jesus. We sat at that same kitchen table in that wonderful house in that northern Ohio town, and I began to share all I knew about Holy Thursday and what happened to Jesus. I didn't stop at Holy Thursday but continued telling all about what Jesus had experienced on Good Friday.

Gradually, as I spoke of the torment and torture Jesus had endured, there was a stirring in me and I began to feel a deep awareness I'd never known before. It grew stronger, and I could not hold back the tears. Realizing that I was not in control, I clearly remember standing up and declaring, "This is just emotional nonsense."

Vivian was with us at the table. She came to me and simply asked, "Are you sure?"

No, I wasn't sure of anything at that point. What gripped me was feeling some amazing empathy for Jesus and what He had endured. Everything changed; from that day forward, my life has never been the same, and I am beyond grateful. I met my savior that evening in my kitchen in that house in Ohio. I began a journey adventure that goes on to this day.

To be clear, at first I didn't realize just what had happened; it took a while to understand and begin to seek Him daily. In the meantime, Vivian had occasion to go to a lecture at Kent State University: it was related to one of our philosopher friends. At the end of the lecture, Mary called me from a pay phone (the way we did it then) to say to me, "Victoria, I know the answer now, and it is Jesus." Yes! And to this day, I will say He is the answer.

Vivian's dedication and devotion to me and my children ranged from the therapy sessions to paying all the bills when I was too sick to work. She helped with cooking and cleaning and being a wonderful friend to Amy, Craig, and Eric. All the while holding down a full-time job in sales at a furniture store.

There came a time when her assignment was completed, and she moved on. I know for certain that God sent Vivian to me. She ministered love and truth to me and stood with me until I truly saw His light.

There were more seasons and people in our lives after Vivian left.

Bag End

Linda J. and her wonderful dog came to live with us, and she was our babysitter who filled many roles very well. To this day, I regret not being able to express my appreciation for all she did. Looking back, I feel as if I took her for granted. She deserved so much more.

The next notable season came about when Hank, who was now out on his own, came to me with this plea. He knew a couple of guys who were sleeping in the laundromat. These were friends of his, and he was concerned for their safety.

The backstory here is the owner of the laundromat was a grouchy woman who owned a gun. Not certain if Hank was concerned, but she would not like them sleeping in her laundromat and might use the gun. This was in the '60s, and homelessness was not a part of the social fabric just yet.

While Vivian and Hank were with me, Vivian named the house Bag End. Yes, right out of *The Hobbit*. Vivian was a fan years before it became popular. I had a roomy house. There were three little ones, a babysitter, her dog, and me, so there was plenty of room for a couple of young men to crash. First three came, and we welcomed them; then another one; and then another. No one was counting, and after all, these were young men who needed a place to live.

So now we we're housing young men between the ages of seventeen and twenty-four. Truth be known, the youngest was sixteen. There was one meeting held before it all became official. We asked Linda if she was okay with having the boys in the house. When she said she was, we set about making some house rules. We had no way of knowing where this was going. If we had—well, I am reminded of the song "Fools Rush In" (where angels fear to tread). While I am convinced Mary had been an angel sent by God, that angel was no longer with me to speak wisdom to me.

As a matter of fact, not only had she moved on—as I mentioned earlier—but since leaving Bag End, she had renewed a friendship with her high school prom date, and they fell in love all over again and were married. In what seemed to me like a reward for the good and sacrificial work she did for me, she went on to live a very interesting part of her journey with this man who had been an important part of her youth.

Back to the present Bag End drama. It wasn't easy to keep track, but as the days went by, it seemed the house filled up with boys who were sleeping over or just hanging out. Rule number one was no drugs: you don't bring them in, and you don't come in if you are high/low from ingesting any. Sometimes someone would show up and announce he had heard about this house. After a little probing on the management's (that being Linda and I) part, he would become a member of this now burgeoning family.

We also had visitors like the young man who came through town with little but his guitar and asked us if he could sing and play for his supper. Linda, who did most of the cooking, agreed. And his rendition of *The Carpenter* was anointed. He was just passing through and left after dinner.

We grew from three originals to eight, but what is difficult to count were the numbers who came on weekends—friends; and friends of friends; and, of course, the dutiful girl friends some of whom took great pains to contribute to the household. Sometimes they helped with cleanup, housework, and cooking; and some brought groceries. We also received monetary gifts from several sources.

Chaos was constant, and crisis visited regularly—the original three soon became a permanent eight males plus; we were very like a large dysfunctional family. Unfortunately, the ones who seem to get lost in the midst of this were my beloved children—Amy, Craig, and Eric.

As time went on, we had some who came from a distance because they had heard about the house. We would probe a bit, and if all seemed right, he would be welcomed into the house. Remember, the head of the house was a single parent who did not know what she was doing. That would be me. I was the so-called head.

Hank commented later that he never thought they would stay, let alone grow in numbers. But when he visited, he was struck how respectful they all were toward me. Frankly, we would not have been able to continue with this arrangement if that were not true.

However, that respect for me didn't change many of the problematic realities. As young men will—these young men, in the era of drug experimentation, took chances and tested the waters of rebellion. Some of the ways it impacted the house were as follows.

Even though they were forbidden to bring drugs into the house and were told never to come home when they were high, those rules did not prevent a very unfortunate episode. A toxic batch of some drug (never did find out what it was) was unleashed in the town. The results were several of our boys were taken to the emergency room. One was picked up by the police, and when they questioned him about Bag End, he told them they had it all wrong because it was not a drug house but a house of friendship; the police let him go.

In the meantime, one member began to manifest symptoms of toxicity at the house. The only one that was home at that time did not drive, but somehow he managed to get the sick one in a car and drive in the snow to the local hospital. Everyone survived.

I was working as secretary to a small business owner. Barely able to keep body and soul together, I somehow managed to feed three children, a live-in baby sitter, myself, and countless of these homeless boys. Every night at our table, we gave thanks and watched the miracle of the loaves and fishes play out before our eyes. Linda was part of that miracle because she did most all of the cooking.

Our phone was tapped, and plain-clothed police visited us in the groups that came on the weekends; but I didn't learn about this until much later. One day, I saw a policeman coming toward me at my office and knew we had another problem. "Your car was involved in an accident." Two of them had taken my car. Most likely a joyride? I don't remember, but when I found out nobody was injured, all I could do was sigh and thank God.

We had a band setup in the basement, and to this day, I marvel when I think of what that must have been like for our neighbors. I owe them an apology and my gratitude. Also, the next-door neighbor's lawn was nearly destroyed by one of the too many cars at Bag End running through their yard, leaving two deep trenches the entire length. These lots had deep front yards, and the unsightly damage to this one was significant. So this was another time I talked with a neighbor who had a legitimate complaint. An agreement was made, and the guilty party made reparations.

As the months wore on, we encouraged the inhabitants of this house to find jobs and help out. That was all well and good, but we didn't realize that some of our young men were working in severe conditions. Avanti had their factory on the outskirts of town. The product used to manufacture the bodies of these cars was composed of fiberglass, and what no one knew at that time was the fibers penetrated the skin. When they came home and showered, the penetration became worse. Just another minor crisis among many major ones.

There is another side of the story. Several of these young men were musically gifted. They appeared professionally as members of bands—two at least were headliners, and one in particular treated us to many wonderful private concerts. I was reminded recently that some of the huge gatherings at the house were fans and groupies. Of course, most were friends and fans and groupies—in that order.

During all this, we got a little paranoid regarding the authorities; of course, it didn't help that most of these inhabitants had varying degrees of paranoia. I was directed to a young attorney who was more than willing to come on board pro bono because he believed we were trying to help. We had some interesting talks about how to protect ourselves against "the big brother" of the day.

As it went on, I clearly had lost control and began to wonder about the goal or even purpose, but I knew no way out. When things seemed overwhelming, a local pastor came into our situation. If I remember correctly, he was with us to help anyone in need of encouragement. As he ministered to all of us, he began to see something: that I was overwhelmed.

What I didn't realize is I was going down; the original purpose and any goals we may have set were also going down. This dear man offered to give me a way out. Frankly, I didn't have a clue how to do that. So at the right time and in the right way, he cleaned house. Then he issued this warning to me, "Do not let anyone in here."

Just before this took place, I had a call from the mayor's office asking if I would meet with him. As it turned out, when the meeting took place, the police chief and city attorney and my attorney and I were all there. I recall them talking to me about what was going on, and eventually they got around to asking if I would call them when one of these runaways would come to my door. I declined, and my attorney said, "That would defeat the purpose." So I think they got it straight: we were there to help the boys and men.

After the dear pastor did his good deed, I found myself having to say no to entire groups of boys coming to the house. It was crazy.

I put the house up for sale. It sold. One memory stands out: a knock on the door at 1:00 a.m., a young man standing on the stoop saying, "Someone told me to come here. I need a place to stay." Then he asked, "Is the owner in?"

I could honestly say, "No, I am sorry, but the owner is not in." We had just closed the sale. I wasn't lying. The owner was not in.

The following are two letters sent from two Bag End alumni a few days ago:

> This is my summary of what Bag End meant to me:
> The decade of the 1960's was closing out and the 1970's 'Twas being ushered in with hopes in a new era. The Vietnam War was still

going strong with no end in sight. The 1960's can only be described as a decade of socio chaos. We witnessed the assassination of JFK, endless race riots, the assassination of Robert Kennedy, Vietnam, and the realization that we were being lied to by our government as to our involvement, the political protests, the beginning of the sexual revolution, bra burning, and the beginning of the feminist movement. Undoubtedly all fuel for skepticism of the pinnacle of post modernism.

The skepticism with fear made me quite the rebellious individual. On the road of self-fulfilling desires and being ruled by 'self' led me to home-lessness, violence, and immorality. That road led me to meet Victoria at her home place called Bag End. There I was to meet various people of various ages and backgrounds who all knew that there was something better than everything we had lived through in the 1960's. Victoria was on a spiritual journey. At first I thought that anything spiritual was for sissies or somehow a cop-out of the weak. But as I watched Victoria's interaction with a bunch of us miscreants (and I use that term lovingly) I noticed the lack of criticisms and judgments by her and the others who either vis-ited Bag End or stayed there. A sort of emotional safe harbor. Victoria was working spiritual ideas and it was affecting the group in positive ways. This was opening the door for me to explore the idea of love (which ultimately Victoria was giv-ing) and the possibility of a real world of spiritual principles. Those of us who remain today still talk about what an impact Victoria and Bag End had on us. Some fifty years later.

Dan D.

Note from Victoria: Of course, what Dan was partaking of was the love of our Lord which has the power to change peoples lives. And letter number 2:

Bag End… Hmmm, what a strange name for a place to live. It was coming on winter 1970. Mickey, Doug, and I were mostly sleeping in the local '24 hour' laundromat. We would keep watch on shifts for the cops while the other two slept. I had just become part of 'the group'. Mickey and Doug hung around down at the Pizza Villa, nights when they were not working. By working I mean Playing, they were both part of the best two bands in town. They would let me hang around because I carried a guitar with me everywhere. I was not that good but could play "Alice's Restaurant 'all the way' so I was cool though my fears told a different story.

I remember the night I was accepted into 'the Friendship', I had just played my nightly version of 'Alice' at the Villa for my free slice of pizza, & fellers asked me if I wanted to go up on Bunker Hill, not the one in Massachusetts, the one at the north end of main street, and drink some beer. I said yeah in my cool voice. I never had beer or any alcohol before. We sat in the grass on Bunker Hill and watched the cars go by.

Then after awhile they said, let's go to the schoolyard and do some orange sunshine and I said yeah. Didn't know what kind of alcohol orange sunshine was but wanted to be cool. Wow, my first night doing alcohol and tried LSD too! Doug, Mickey, and I got back to the laundromat just before daylight and I was surprised to hear them say "we have to stop doing this". I was thinking, are you out of your minds, we need to do more of this! They were referring mostly to living in a laundromat. It just so happened we ran into my buddy Keith that day. Keith and I played in a wanna-be band together. We were talking about staying in the laundromat and he said he might know a lady that would let us crash at her place a few days. Her name was Victoria and she lived at Bag End…

Bag End for me became a few years, for Mickey and Doug kinda that also. Victoria invited us in and I don't remember if there were any time restrictions which soon melted away if there were. The agreement was don't bring any drugs into the house. I have no clue how difficult that all was for her.

I've only begun to understand in much later years how irresponsible we were and how giving she was. I remember nights I would play my guitar sitting on the kitchen counter while we all would sing, and laugh and tell stories. Many more people came. I met two friends that are in my life still today. I remember Boo and I playing Wooden Ships by CNS&Y in the living room in front of the fireplace. Mickey would help us with harmonies. I remember building my Triumph motorcycle in the basement and running through Boo's drums when I first started it up cause my clutch cable broke. Boo laughed while he sat there on the washing machine. There were many times like that.

Bag End was a time in my life, to quote a favorite song writer, "when the roads were as many as the places I had dreamed of and my friends and I were one". I remember conversations with Victoria at the kitchen table about being aware of my spiritual life. Didn't know what that was or

If I had one, but she helped me to think in those ways in those days. Today I know Victoria as the person who set me on my spiritual path... What a blessing.

Rocky

New England Chapter

So onto Massachusetts: after much searching and realizing that my parents made their move and did not invite me to go west with them, east to New England was in our sites; and we went with it.

Two childhood dreams were fulfilled when we settled into our lovely new home (condo by the sea). One to live in New England, and the other to live on the ocean. Such an overwhelming gratitude came to me at the realization.

I read books as a girl that were written about New England or the setting was New England, and I was mesmerized by the descriptions. And, of course, doesn't everyone want to live where the ocean beach is their front yard. Just a little piece of heaven on earth. The Northern MA shore was breathtaking. Just up the road from our beachfront home was New Hampshire, and I learned to love that state.

A more important reality set in as we made our home in that little hamlet. It was actually, as you might have guessed, a resort area. The turning toward my three children at this point was most needed. They had endured a confusing and nearly neglectful experience when the boys of Bag End ruled the day. It was about a year and a half before we were forced to quit that lifestyle and move on to a place to enjoy as a family. And enjoy we did!

Aside from the breathtaking beauty of the New England countryside, an amazing amount of history lived amidst all those towns and in many of those buildings. It was perfect for a young family with limited means and adventuresome attitudes.

On any given day, I would pull out the familiar picnic basket and announce where we were going that day, or pose to the children what they would like to see. There was such a variety of interesting sites we never ran short of after nearly three years of exploring. Think of visiting the Revolutionary War historical places, including Paul Revere's house, and the church where colonists met before they boarded the ship in Boston Harbor for a tea party of renown.

Then you had the House of Seven Gables made famous by Nathaniel Hawthorne's novel. Of course, all the reminiscence of Salem and the infamous witch trials was celebrated. Then Plymouth, where the Rock was and on and on. We never ran out of fun places to visit. Then there was the ocean, beach, mountains, Cape Cod, and Cape Ann—all jewels in this crown. Fortunately, my children enjoyed all this, including museums chock-full of historical goodies. And all this was barely scratching the surface.

It could not have been a more perfect place to reconcile with and devote myself to my children. Add to this the school in this town was absolutely the finest I had ever known and proved the finest Amy and Craig would ever attend. There was actually no accounting for this in the normal course of events; somehow this amazing school was part of a small and somewhat simple community in this rather obscure Massachusetts village, which incidentally was visited by Washington and Lafayette during The War. The women of Salisbury gave all their pewter items to help in furnishing the colonials with ammunition.

On the subject of the school, Craig had two teachers who became family friends. In both cases, the wives were his teacher, but both husbands and wives became close family friends. This was especially helpful to the children who didn't have the attention of a father. I still think fondly of those two young couples, and it is sad that we have lost track of them.

New England culture is unique. Although we have been gone a long time, I clearly remember being aware that the townspeople were standoffish. They evaluated you at a distance. If you passed their scrutiny and became accepted, they couldn't be warmer or more supportive. I was medical assistant to the local doctor, and in that capacity, the vetting process was probably accelerated. Just for your information, Salisbury population is around five thousand. Still a very small town.

We had a Thanksgiving at the beach that was memorable—a nor'easter blew in that day, and the power blew away; the turkey was literally undone by that, and if my memory serves me, we ate sometime near the middle of the night.

I was working at Andover Inn during that season, and another blizzard created so much havoc I could not get home from work for two days. Conveniently I was able to get a room at the inn. On the other hand, I scrambled to find a way to rescue my children. The real estate agent, who found the oceanfront condo for us, came to the aid of the three little ones who needed to get to safety—away from the ocean front.

When I drove home a few days following that storm, there were mounds of sand and snow that had blown on to the roadway where we lived. And the buildings—cottages and condos—look as if they had been sandblasted, but it was snow and ice not sand in this case.

The following spring, we moved in with our dear friend Sandy J, who lived in a second-floor apartment in a house in the middle of the woods. And while it was cramped inside, the woods offered an adventure unlike the ocean but still intriguing, so the children were treated to another lifestyle.

The in-the-woods experience ended, we returned to the oceanfront for another season, and finally landed in a property on a farm. We occupied the second and third floor of the farmhouse. This was a large colonial that was divided down the middle.

There was a story about two brothers who occupied the house generations before and had a serious falling out; so they literally built a brick wall down the middle of the house. They lived in the divided house but had nothing to do with each other. One wall of the living room where we lived stood as testament to that story; it was red brick.

This was a unique opportunity for the children to experience farm life without having the responsibility of a farm family. It was truly a remarkable time for all four of us.

There came a day when an ad appeared in the newspaper, following an extraordinary Christmas celebration—and they are all extraordinary in New England. (Nothing quite like it.) This year, for some reason, the Christmas tree selection was put off until just a few days before the big day. The scraggly tree we found was reminiscent of Charlie Brown's tree. We brought it home, decorated it in the finest, and decided to love it in all its (no one said this out loud) ugliness. It actually began to appear lovely the longer we had it in the living room. And it goes without saying that was a very memorable Christmas with my children.

Back to the ad—United Airlines was offering a deal for a flight from Boston to San Francisco too good to pass up. No coincidence, I had a heart tug a few weeks before. I was really missing my dad. So we booked the flight, family friends took care of my children, and I was on my way.

When I returned after time with my parents and brothers, I knew we were destined to move to California. And it was a sooner-than-later reality.

During our time in New England, we lived on the ocean, in the woods, and finally on a farm. All these experiences were wonderful for this family. But not until we came to California did we ever have sidewalks—a interesting piece of trivia.

California Chapter

Ah! California! The Golden State, and it was looking good when we landed in the southland after moving lock, stock, barrel, and bicycles across the country. The bicycles had to be removed from the trunk/rack every night before we could get to the suitcases and into the motel room at the end of each day.

After driving many miles, the nuisance of lugging two bicycles from car to room and back to car was, at best, annoying. The rack required lashing those bikes securely. I don't know why that seems significant. Perhaps it was symbolic of the lugging all this travel took. I hasten to add we loved seeing all the grand wonderfulness of our country as we traveled from coast to coast. But nothing could have prepared us (in a good way) for the beauty of the coast of California—in a word, magnificent.

Many contrasts between California and New England culture. Some were evident immediately. The young people of our neighborhood in Salisbury, Massachusetts, had befriended us and were respectful; the first indication that wasn't so in California was driving through one of the middle-class neighborhoods in Livermore. Coming upon a group of young people in the street who were playing ball, they yelled profanities as we inched our way through. It proved to be true: these young people exhibited entitlement you would never find in good ole New England.

And on the other hand, a friendliness across the board in California was spontaneous and acceptance didn't need to be earned. California was eager to help and offered me, as the single mother of three, many benefits. While it was part of the political and social climate in California, in New England it was individually driven. I can't tell you how many people reached out to me in that little hamlet in New England when they learned of our situation.

In mid-1970s, not too many single/divorced parents were out there. New England people seemed more private (some would say reserved); California people were more open and inclusive. Just a few of the differences we experienced.

Our first home in California was lovely, and we made some wonderful family memories there—not to mention for the very first time in my children's lives, they had sidewalks in front of the house. Some things can only be experienced on a sidewalk.

In this time of family history came some of the most challenging with my sons. It went from their very creative and interesting offenses to very serious matters of destruction. They developed unmanageable activities.

Eric was transitioning from fearless antics—such as climbing the tallest trees wherever he was and swinging back and forth while holding onto the highest branch to climbing on roofs and tossing shingles from that house into the swimming pool, finally destroying the filter-system. He went from leaning two-inch nails against each tire of my car so that when I backed out of the driveway to take him to school, all four tires went flat to setting fire to the neighbor's fence, resulting in nearly burning down the house.

And then there were the weekly calls from Eric's teacher telling me of his very distracting behaviors. Eric always had a way of entertaining the other children, be they fellow students or his siblings. The kids loved it; the adults not so much.

Craig drew away from the family and managed to find areas of great influence; none to good. He kept most of his activities away from the neighborhood. Craig was a leader, and he was clever. So I wasn't as aware of much of what he was into. But from time to time, something would happen to let me know we were in trouble.

Eric did not ever seem to be malevolent, although some things had very bad consequences. On the other hand, Craig was a leader and was more sophisticated. They each wreaked havoc in ways I don't care to write about.

Need I add, I had lost control.

All the while, Amy managed to enjoy her friends and her dance; she was a student of ballet from age twelve on, and she was faithful to the discipline. I believe she enjoyed it.

Craig and Eric participated in sports usually organized by a city league or church: basketball and soccer respectively. I found myself having to be at two places at the same time, one of the feats of a single parent. And yes, it is not possible.

In fourth grade, Eric's teacher was at her wits end and would call me every Friday evening to report on his antics in the classroom. I listened patiently and sympathized, but who was I to have any suggestions? The entire situation was beyond me. So listening is all I did until I invited her to dinner at our home. Was it somewhere between a bribe and an empathetic gesture? Probably, but it really didn't change anything—the weekly calls continued.

I was left with no solution, until one day I thought perhaps we could put Eric into a private school. So his father agreed to pay tuition to a Christian School, and the problem grew more complex. His new teacher was married to a police officer who assessed Eric's behavior as that of one who seems to be prison bound.

After two years of patient trying, the verdict was reached: the principal called me to say they could no longer keep Eric in their school. Spare me the reasons; I was through listening to all the complaints. However, I called the Youth Pastor at the church we were attending at that time, and his suggestion was that daughter Amy (Eric's older sister) and I would start praying for Eric and this new situation fervently. That would be with perseverance and faith.

The school stopped calling, and at the graduation ceremony six months later, Eric received the Overcomer's Award. Talk about an answer to prayer.

There are many more stories of raising the children in California, but I think you get the idea.

Of course, the times of adulthood: Amy married, Craig started a business (after training for deep-sea diving), and Eric and I were alone together in a new house.

After all those changes, the most profound change came about.

"I Must Be Crazy!"

My father died, and that began an unbelievable, unimaginable journey that changed everything I ever knew, thought I knew, or believed.

The normal shock and grief—I thought I was getting through.

This is how it happened. A few days after his eighty-fourth birthday, early in the morning, my mother called to say my father was not responding; she agreed to call 911, and we headed to the hospital. I was eventually told there was no hope and that I could see him in a room by myself.

I spent time in that room with him singing a song to him. As I did, a tear came from his eye and down his face. Then I couldn't bear to be there anymore, and I left. My brother followed me into the room and, within a few minutes, came out to say Papa was gone.

I expected to grieve and mourn, cry and hurt. Regret and guilt set in early in the process because I had left him while he was dying. I couldn't get past that. It took years, and finally someone said to me, "Did you ever think that your father wanted to spare you the sorrow of seeing him die?" Finally I could live with that possibility.

So I took on the grieving; he died in June, and by September, I began to experience daily fevers and other symptoms—never quite sick enough to seek medical help but obviously not functioning normally. Then I began to have great difficulty getting out of bed. I don't have a detailed recall here, but I felt very disconnected from everything and everyone.

Trying to get back to work after the fevers ceased was not going well. Now I was struggling to get up in the morning plus the inexplicable crying and sobbing began each morning as I attempted to get ready for work. Day after day, and soon the battle took on another phase—the guilt and fear, and thinking about anything other than how I had completely failed.

The inevitable fatigue, lack of concentration, and deep sadness led to belief I needed therapy to help me over this depression. Then it was thought to be reactive depression due to the loss of my father. There were some interesting experiences at that time: I clearly remember falling into something for which I have no description. I can tell you it was consuming; the rest is such a myriad of feelings, but it was horrible. And even as I write this, my stomach is churning—nausea. I was compelled to walk and walk, truly driven to walk until some relief would come; I'm talking about actual physical walking, and then I could continue with life.

And then therapy. After several sessions, the therapist declared he couldn't help me. This is in spite of the fact I was diagnosed and medicated accordingly. During the next fifteen years, at least sixteen mental health professionals tried, but most were unable to put Humpty Dumpty back together again. That child's nursery rhyme played over and over in my mind all the while. It became more meaningful as more memory unfolded. There were, however, three professional therapists who did help. Truly amazing people, and I am grateful to this day for them.

This history is hard to recall; it was intense and chaotic. The sense of failure permeated and began to affect everything. Withdrawal was a necessary stance, and so—left with all these symptoms, including losing ground every day—I became a recluse. Concentration was nearly impossible, so I no longer was able to read.

Now everything stopped. A certain unawareness set in; either I was unable to perform or didn't recognize the need to do anything. Slipping into this unreality, one memory stands out. Seemingly losing contact with my surroundings, I would often find myself in peculiar places and inexplicable postures.

One such time I came to in my bedroom, lying on the floor, amidst mounds of unopened mail. The distress was serious and I felt as if I couldn't lift my head. As I lie there, I saw something out of the corner of my eye. Trying to understand what this was, I struggled to clear my vision; and there, in the midst of my being down on the floor, I could see two shoes just there. Not moving; no sound.

When I finally was able to take it in, there in the middle of this mess—in the middle of what looked like collapse—stood my teenage son. All that I could feel from him was a caring that he could not express except to be there; he was there.

It followed that he was there many times for me in ways that, to this day, amaze me.

Another way the trouble came was flashes of memory that made no sense, but the power would send me into a frenzy. I would try desperately to get away from whatever that was trying to get me: that picture in my mind that made no sense but had immense power.

Then someone told me about a therapist they knew; her name was D. Miller, and she became one of the amazing and ultimately successful three I referred to earlier. She and I entered into a new chapter together. She was, in my life, an angel; a true helper; and, to this day, a friend. I could spend days telling of this woman's heart, not to mention her insights, wisdom, and commitment. In a very long list of professionals, she was the true professional and more, much more.

There emerged three interesting experiences. I had enough stability at one time to begin reading again. And since no one had been able to ascertain what was happening to me, I devoured everything written that resembled what I had been going through.

In one of those *aha!* moments, I came across information regarding PTSD symptoms. It was very much what I knew for myself. The second was a very peculiar inner voice stating clearly, *Your father molested you.* And the third was a memory flash of my father in a position that supported the statement he was incestuous. Added to this was a disturbing memory that played over in my mind throughout my life, one in which I was being abused by a female relative. Like so much that I was beginning to experience, this was visceral. To this day, my body reacts to this memory.

The mantra I lived with for some time was, "you must be crazy" playing over and over in my mind. This was the beginning of a downward spiral into darkness beyond imagining. Let me emphasize nothing could have prepared me for the truth that was uncovered.

I clearly remember telling D. Miller many times that I wish I could lose my mind. Somehow, insanity seemed comforting. As I went through the next ten years and uncovered multiple diagnoses, I wasn't afforded the escape that insanity would have brought, or so I believed.

"Humpty Dumpty" repeated in my mind in those days—he had a great fall, and all the king's horses and all the king's men (the professional men and women) could not put Humpty together again.

I had been a faithful church-goer and enjoyed the community and the service very much. I clearly remember the Sunday when I went to the entrance of the church, could hear the music, but was not able to enter. It was as if some invisible force was in front of me; I could not get past it.

And then there's this: the outward manifestation of what was happening came when I came to—this time, cowered in a corner of my small bathroom curled up, so as to hide myself, pleading with God not to look at me. Crying and sobbing and asking, "Please don't look at me" over and over again. Trying desperately to disappear.

The awareness of this despicable person—me who was far beyond worthless, loathsome, evil—was a precursor to the reality I had entered into. I think somewhere near this time I began to have fantasies of cutting my arms and derived pleasure in fantasizing my blood running down my arms, watching with relief and relish while the life poured out of my body.

During this time I found myself drawn impulsively to sharp objects, i.e. razor blades. The impulse was to become a compulsion and engaged in actual cutting before I was to have relief and, eventually, overcome the inner drive to use these cutting tools. Often the guilt accompanying those days, while I was used to living with guilt, was something I never knew existed.

I must admit I was to go to places of emotion, pain, and horror in every sense of the word that I never knew existed, the intensity which would then often drive me to a kind of madness. I began to develop other symptoms of deep-seated problems: agoraphobia and panic attacks joined the suicidal ideation. I was locked down in a psychiatric hospital at one point and spent that time verbally attacking one of the doctors. His behavior was that of a perpetrator.

My idea of therapy had been you talk, tell it all, and the therapists helps you understand yourself; and while there might be some difficulties accepting the truth, you could go home and work with it until the next session. I was to learn that there was much more to it, and depending on the amount of trauma, it could be extremely difficult.

Sessions with my therapist were like battles. I managed to know part of a memory just enough to get the turmoil started; sometimes it was a thought or picture in my mind that started a series of highly charged feelings that would take over. Involuntarily, often I found myself moving about the room, usually scooting across the floor or crawling like a two-year-old trying to get away; it was difficult to understand just what was happening. Completely out of control, the body would taken over.

Many times, I seemed unable to stay in the room; that is, conscious of what was happening. The shaking and screaming were overwhelming. At these times, pressure would build and build until it felt as if I would surely explode—and explode is exactly what would happen, and with great force. This is what was going on while I was in various stages of awareness.

I do clearly remember the first real memory of my father's molest. The picture in my mind would start the process of remembering; I had been visited by this picture many times, and while strong and fearful feelings began to surface, the battle would begin. Then often there were screams from somewhere inside me as I relived the trauma. In therapy, the defenses would give way, and the full impact of what had happened to me would come through my body with such force.

I realize this illustration has been used to describe many experiences. It is, in the purist form, true in telling of these experiences. The volcano begins to rumble and shake, and the rumbling and shaking can be very devastating; then it begins to spew forth that which is deep inside.

That volcano can lay quiet and dormant for many years; in a way, storing energy, the force of which blows the lava many miles into the air. This is very like what I experienced in this therapy. Only it was my body that held the quiet lava, and it was my body that exploded when the truth pierced the quiet lava—in this case, memory of serious trauma.

So much was going on with the body, mind, and soul; one was left exhausted only to learn this was the beginning of the process.

As it turned out, many years of retrieving buried memories were ahead of me. The molest of my father was just the beginning.

Myriad of physical symptoms and many hospitalizations occurred over the next several years. And while doctors attempted to diagnose, the symptoms—which on many occasions seemed serious and were accompanied by clinical findings—would seem to fade or disappear. In a way, there was a counterpart, mentally and psychologically, in that I was diagnosed with many different mental disorders. All was chaotic in these matters. In the early times, nothing was defined.

Moving through what I have come to refer to as "the process," I encountered more and more strange triggers and somatic distresses. The body holds on to memories and releases them without warning. At a time and place when the memory—which has been held in both mind and body—decides it is time to release, one loses control.

At the mercy of triggers, one finds reactions which are very strong and unpredictable. Once, while watching a TV show, there was a scene depicting an intruder entering a sleeping woman's bedroom. As I watched that scene develop, I was very suddenly overtaken by an emotional outburst, and immediately my body began to convulse.

The next awareness I had was a sensation that my body was twisting slowly, as if something on the inside was turning my spine like a slow twist. These experiences are difficult to describe. Fear and pain, both physical and emotional, accompany these.

I became agoraphobic and had a panic disorder, to name a few. One therapist thought I was bipolar; everyone agreed I was clinically depressed, which then became chronic. I believed there was some borderline tendencies in there as well.

Then there was the anger. This emotion nearly took over during "the process." Fear and grief and shock were chief among feelings for most of the early years, but then there was anger. More like rage.

One of the many ways this was expressed was classic road rage. I became overcome with fierce anger anytime someone would cross me while driving. Immediately I would pursue the offender. Sometimes just waiting for an opportunity to get them, or actually speeding down the road to catch them. Only in retrospect did I identify the danger in that behavior and also realized how much I was that driver that I had watched in disgust before; I had become one of them.

Another way I expressed this is in relationships. If I disagreed with someone, they became a target of outrageous attacks, withering tirades until I saw them as defeated foes and me employing perpetrator tactics. Some justifying relief set in when the target shrunk back.

There was always a cauldron of rage, but it was limited to expression in environments that were safe. Unfortunately, that would be the closest ones in my life: children. While at the time I would feel justified because it seemed this anger bordering rage was always because I was frustrated by the others behavior.

I've learned coming through to the other side of this process. Much of this dire behavior was directly connected to trauma I had suffered, the effects of which were stored inside of me. What I later, much later, learned is that this was now in the psychic bloodstream of my children—also, a spiritual reality set in.

There is reason we were endowed with the emotion of anger. As with all emotions, they are important signals that, when appropriate, actually serve us well. However, as with all things in our nature, the operative word should be *self-control*, but someone who is very damaged has little control. Or another person may control to the point of denying these strong feelings when seemingly inappropriate. There is a price to pay for that also. The help comes in the form of getting healthy, but for some, that is a very hard and long road. Trust me, it is worth it.

Back to triggers. They can prove very embarrassing, particularly when one goes off in a public setting. The psychological definition is a smell, sound, sight, or even anniversary date that sets off a memory or flashback, transporting the person back to the event of her/his original trauma. I tend to think there is a lot more to what sets them off.

There are a few that, I recall, were very inopportune. One at a restaurant where I was having dinner with a friend—without any warning, something was set off and the rest was chaotic. The police were called. When they got there, I was returning slowly to reality, and the young police officer said he had been in training for just such a behavior the week prior. They did not arrest me; I created a disturbance but did no harm otherwise.

Another was at a dinner party with family and friends. I was listening to the conversation at the table and suddenly felt they were in another reality. They could not ever understand my world or what we (people of the trauma) went through. Feeling totally detached from them, all began a downward spiral and finally had to be helped out of the place where the dinner was to take place.

Fortunately, my daughter was there to rescue me. The last one was in a retail store; again I lost it. Not much memory about what took place, just that awareness that you were out of control and in another place in your mind.

Back to the journey. It seemed we were getting through the portion of my therapeutic journey relating to my father's molest. We learned that my mother undoubtedly knew. But what was to come would astound and take me once again to the place of disbelief: I must be crazy. There was no way to believe what was being uncovered without wondering that I was crazy to think that these two people I thought I knew were indeed the two people who raised me. Then my mother died in 1986 at age eighty-two; anything left of normalcy was shattered with memories that began to surface with unbelievable content.

Not only did my mother know, but she participated in the molest with my father. Clear-and-defining memories surfaced. No one wants such a thing to be true. Much of this time has faded in my memory, except the memory of this devastating trauma.

As I write this, glimpsing the memory, I feel a sickness in me. At this point in the process, I clearly felt that I had no parents. The sense of being orphaned became a reality. Any sense of being safe in the world was gone. Ontologically, there was no place to land—aimless drifting. Little did I know the worst was yet to come.

An amazing intensity burst on the scene in my therapy, just when it seemed there could not be any worse remembrances. The first was of a small child—a girl who was in a white dress—and she was being abused beyond anything I had known; and I was watching it. I didn't recognize her, but she was probably about five years old. What was being done to her was unspeakable in cruelty, culminating in her death.

This began a year's long recollection, which I have decided to tell by describing three or four incidents to inform; but these three or four such memories represent many such experiences. While I know it is incredibly important to tell this part of the family's story, I have chosen to keep the telling of this horror to a minimum. Not to protect my family, but to protect you, the reader, from undue assault.

Item number one: my brother Goeff (this was happening when we were children) was being sexually abused by these people (and there were more than my parents involved), and again I was forced to watch.

Item number two: routinely, I was held captive in a cage and was subject to intentional near-drowning attempts at the hands of a group of very evil people.

And lastly, I was raped more than one time and was ultimately impregnated. I have reason to believe my brother was the father of this baby, which was born and was subsequently murdered.

By this time, some of you may recognize the abuse as satanic, which it was. The same aunt who abused me in my home was one of the chief participants. Curious caveat: she was also my godmother.

My mother was a victim of their severe abuse, brainwashing, and programming as a child. I believe my father was blackmailed by them. Of course, that is all very convenient, but the truth is these people operate this way and, for the most part, do so with impunity.

I choose not to tell of the many evidences of such activities, but I will tell this. There came a time following my father's death when my mother confessed to my brother: "This family has been involved in something so evil." She said she would tell him about it—that never happened; however, it is good that she left that confession for her children-victims: my siblings and me.

My brother Goeff murdering his baby now understood in light of this history. My brother Ed suffering diabetes which, in my estimation, was trauma-induced. Ed also would later tell me of nightmares so terrorizing he became afraid to fall asleep. Many of these had very similar scenes of severe abuse.

Another interesting fact: my sister Rose was spared the direct involvement in all this. I know there is an explanation for this. She may well have been a bargaining chip.

"You, Marie, can have this firstborn. And we will take the others, providing they meet our criteria," I can hear them tell my mother.

While it would seem significant that Rose was spared, the family system was so contaminated that all were infected, even the one who was spared the horrific abuse. By perfect design, the family is a unit; and as such, each member is affected by the other and, most especially, by those in authority—the parents. This rests in the physical, psychological, and most importantly, spiritual—all are impacted by all and again, especially the parents.

This is not meant to be an exposé. I could furnish information to substantiate what I am writing here, but I have reasons for telling this story that have nothing to do with proving what I have lived.

The Miraculous

Please, God, onto the good news—you might even say the amazing news. When we left off the family members' stories earlier in this account, including parents, they were at different places in their lives. Let me tell you how each one fared.

My sister, Rose, is ninety-three years old and is still in charge of her faculties. As I mentioned earlier, her son—Jamie—lives in the Florida home that she and her husband, Gene, bought many years ago, and together they manage to have a good life there.

Rose and our mother had a special relationship throughout her marriage. Rose maintained a telephone relationship with our mother in which they talked every Saturday morning, and this—without fail—continued for years. What is so good now is that Rose and I have continued that tradition. (And it is far more than a tradition.)

Shortly after our mother's death in 1986, we began to honor that commitment, now to each other. So for the past thirty-four years, we have been meeting on the telephone, usually Saturday morning, for two hours. We never run out of important things to discuss.

Our brother Goeff lived a full life in Northern California following his incarceration. He met the perfect woman and married her. She was so encouraging to him. She was exactly what he needed to navigate adult life. He was active in the Big Brother organization. He continued his involvement in chess and taught young people in his community to play. He was a projectionist at the local theater; something he learned while in Huntsville. And most importantly, he was a wonderful father figure to my son Craig and, to some extent, to my son Eric as well. I am so grateful to Goeff and his wife, Liz, for filling in this place so well.

Then came the final sorrow of Goeff's life. Diagnosed with cancer, we managed to eek out some very important times together, and I believe others in his life did as well. We spent many afternoons just enjoying each other and sometimes forgetting what we faced. But I feel we were learning to face it together.

The final act was like a story from the Bible. Goeff's Jewish mother-in-law was staying with her daughter Liz and son-in-law, Goeff. The time came when a Catholic priest was summoned to administer the last sacrament to Goeff as he was near the end. The priest came to the house, prayed over my brother, and got up to leave. It was then that his Jewish mother-in-law stopped the priest at the door and said, "This man needs to know he has been forgiven." The priest immediately went back to my brother's side and, armed with the information his mother-in-law provided, prayed a new and very important prayer.

And then there's Edward, my beloved younger brother. He, like Goeff, found a wife that has been by his side now for over forty years. He managed to keep body and soul together for them for many years. Meg, his wife, was a helpmate and still is. She worked hard for many years to help with furnishing some very important survivals.

By the way, these two sisters-in-law were loyal and faithful and most helpful.

Then one Christmas Eve, Ed decided to go to church. As far as I know, he hadn't been to a service in any church for many years. That Christmas Eve, he walked into a little church in his town, and as he entered, something very extraordinary occurred. He would later describe it as amazing, life-changing—a sense of the presence of God. He has never been the same. And from this place, he gave his heart and life to the Lord Jesus.

Now for the most remarkable of all, the miraculous. I came to California believing in part I was there to at least speak to my parents about their spiritual state if not lead them to know the God of their salvation.

I prayed and watched and waited for an opening, but after a few years, I was still waiting for the opportunity. Finally, my Papa was taken to the hospital, and after visiting him there, Mama and I spent some time together at their home.

So this seemed to be the time I was waiting for. But when I spoke the message of Jesus, Mama spoke to me these words, "Oh, I did that during a televised Billy Graham Crusade in the living room at our home." After I started breathing again, I began talking about Papa, to which she answered, "Oh, your father knows the Lord." Never had I known anybody to be so certain of anything as my mama was about her husband's spiritual condition and hers as well.

Those readers who understand the implications of all of this will know as I do, without a doubt, my entire family (Rose is making her way) have had their salvation before they left this earth.

If you are looking for miracles, look no further. This is an extraordinary family of miracles. Only our God could have worked in such unbelievable ways.

The darkness we were in, the Lord Himself penetrated—His light overcame that deep darkness. He saved those who seemed to have no hope. He undid the enemy's hold on these and brought them into His Kingdom. Let this be encouraging to any who are wondering about loved ones. He left the ninety-nine to rescue the one. In this case, it was a whole family.

You may have some lost sheep in your family, but He is the perfect Good Shepherd.

The Other Journey

Come with me on a parallel journey of much importance. As a very young child, I made friends with God. I intuitively knew He was there and spent many hours telling Him everything I thought was important to tell. Never doubting He heard me, nothing else mattered. I didn't need manifestations; I just knew He was there.

That explains what I am about to tell you. A memory surfaced during my adult life. Remembering, at some point as a child in all the craziness, I said to my friend, "You know what's happening, and that is all that matters." The remarkable thing is that *I* knew God's knowing was enough. That, I believe, is miraculous.

When I walked the walk of elementary school years, much of my memory is lost; however, what I do recall is, again, most unusual. During these years, I spent many summer mornings going to mass at the Catholic Church more than a mile away from my home. It never seemed sacrificial in the truest sense of the word. But I was aware that my friends were not interested in mass when they could sleep in during the summer vacation they so richly deserved. I don't recall feeling superior, just satisfied.

Another way my heart showed up in grade school. While it was not an easy time for me, as with many children, I never felt accepted by most of my peers. Somehow I didn't relate or fully understand what was expected of me by my peers. I managed to develop a few friendships, but for the most part, I was an outsider.

When the other children were on the playground at noon in recess, many times you would find me in the empty church. By this time, I had developed a vivid imagination and would fantasize spiritual visitations. However, I now believe I was drawn to the comfort of a spiritual reality. God was with me.

Becoming a nun was something many young Catholic girls of my generation considered, and I was one of that many. I clearly remember watching the postulates in my freshman year in an all-girls Catholic academy with admiration, but as the year went on, I became uninterested in that austere expression. I think the world was becoming more interesting to me.

I was fascinated by the many adult relationships that were developing for me. In time, I was totally caught up in teenage activity. While those were more tame than what takes place with teens in these times, I was deep into worldly behaviors. Admittedly, memories are sketchy for many of these years; there are enough to indicate I was moving away from my very conscious spiritual journey.

It was during my eighteenth summer that a very significant decision was made. I read a book entitled *This is my beloved*. The first-ever written by a Carmelite nun. This order was so dedicated to the Lord they were cloistered; they removed themselves from society and spent most of their time in prayer. I was wanting to join that order at one time.

The book was amazing and told the story from inside the convent. That convent was located in downtown New York. The only contact these nuns had with outside was an opening in the wall that was around the grounds of the convent where people could put prayer requests written on pieces of paper. The nuns would retrieve those requests by opening a door on their side of the opening. The requesters had a door to open on their side, enabling them to place their petitions inside the opening on the wall.

At one time, that sounded wonderful to me. However, as I sat in the family cottage that summer day and finished that book, some friends came to my door. I clearly remember thinking I have a choice:

I can go with them, or I can go deeper into the Carmelite world. I very deliberately chose my friends.

And away I went into the world of excitement and, amazingly, one of acceptance. There were delicious experiences that kept me occupied for years. It happens that many young people, not having any sense of who they are, get swept away by every whim and get lost—sometimes very lost. That is the simple explanation for a very complex part of my life. Marked with choices that took me further away and into dangerous and sometimes dark places, this chapter in my life was ugly.

Many a night, as I faced the pillow on my bed, I was besieged with guilt, but it would be gone in the morning only to meet me the next night. I never questioned what I was doing, or who I had become. I just continued to follow the path to more lostness and more guilt. Don't know what I thought was going to happen, but now I believe God was protecting me in the time when I was neither acknowledging Him nor willing to look at myself.

Stage left: enter Josh and, if you remember, the rest of this story was his loving rescue and ultimate abandonment. However, there was a new story out of that pain. That story is the one I am telling now: Jesus came and everything changed, and we never returned to the other but went on into a wonderful relationship with my Lord that has been incredible, miraculous, and I could go on. Let me take you along this path.

Yes, I was a single mom of three. Yes, I did not know what I was doing when it came to parenting. And despite trials and testing that I thought would break me at times, there was Jesus alongside and, in fact, by His Spirit actually in me. That fact is one that takes faith to walk—spirit of the living God living in me. Most of the time I just took a step at a time and prayed my way through.

It is difficult to relate how many times and ways I experienced the Lord while I struggled to be the parent. He provided in ways I can't begin to enumerate, but be assured they were happening all the time. Financially I watched Him bring provision when there seemed to be no way, always on time. And yes, I was a working mother; but while I know the jobs I had were from His hand, I saw Him bring help, augmenting whatever that job paid so that we were often on the edge but never over that edge and off the cliff.

My favorite scripture in that season was, "Seek ye first the Kingdom of God and His righteousness and all these other things will be added unto you" Matthew 6:33 (NLT). It has been true in my life, time after time.

Then there was the matter of need of direction and fellowship. How beautifully He met that. He sent teachers to my children who were Christian, and two of them and their husbands became friends of this family. He sent coworkers who became fast friends and amazing spiritual support. We began to attend a church as a family, and the pastor and wife became close friends and ministered to my family.

And then, wonder of wonders, someone told me about a prayer meeting the likes of which I had never heard. It was taking place in a monastery in New Hampshire. It was a game changer in every way. Between fifty and a hundred people gathered and spent much of the time praising and worshipping God out loud and singing to Him.

Then a person would stand up in the meeting and tell what the Lord had done for them in practical and sometimes miraculous ways. I learned later that this was at the prompting of the Holy Spirit. Another would stand to proclaim a truth the Lord was telling them in that moment. Didn't know it at the time, but this was prophecy.

Another would stand to tell that someone in the group assembled had a problem or disease or something that they were troubled with; the person standing would call out the problem and give a word of encouragement or even an answer or a word of healing. This was a manifestation of the gift known as a word of knowledge, described in the Bible as another gift of the Holy Spirit. Invariably, someone in the meeting would acknowledge the *word* that had been spoken in the assembly was for them.

It was amazing, and I couldn't get enough of what was happening there every Friday evening.

Some of you may recognize this as the move of the Holy Spirit that has come to be known as the charismatic renewal. The various manifestations were indeed the gifts of the Holy Spirit operating among the body of believers. It was holy, it was awe inspiring, and it was transforming. And it was just what I needed. I received the baptism of the Holy Spirit. For me, it was a life-changing step into God in a way I had not known before. I have never been the same, and I would never want to go back.

With newfound faith and vigor, my life took on a strength and purposefulness that was simply ordained by God I have no doubt. I was living a spiritual reality that caused a closer experience with Jesus. As I began to seek the way from here, I discovered a prayer meeting in the local Catholic Church. I became very involved with the supplications and petitions of that weekly prayer group and also with the participants.

On the wall in my kitchen was a chalkboard I used to write the names of the people I was praying for. When I would learn of an answer, I would erase the name. Of course, some names remained longer than others.

I worked for the town general practitioner, and he was friends with the pharmacist in town. At one point, he ask for prayer, and so he was on my board. When his friend, the doctor, came to my house, he saw the pharmacist's name on the chalkboard.

Dr. H. must have told him that he was on the prayer board because when I was in the pharmacy—shopping—from behind the pharmacy counter, he (the pharmacist) shouted to me several aisles away, "Take my name off that prayer list of yours. I have been having nothing but trouble." I never knew if my friend, the pharmacist, was wrestling with God, or if this was an exercise in humbling me. I rather think it probably was the latter; it could have been both.

When I had carefully shared with a friend about the amazing ways that God worked in my life and gently led her to a place of curiosity, it was disconcerting to have her say to me, "If you really believe all you say about the Lord in your life, why do you smoke?" I did not have an answer, but I was completely aware how foolish this was. I had stopped smoking several times in the past only to start again when the going got rough.

These words from this friend pierced all my defenses. I knew I could no longer speak this way to anyone and continue in my addiction. This is a purely personal experience, and I don't pretend to have answers for all persons caught in any addictions whatsoever. However, I view this woman's challenge as the method God used to get my attention in a way that hadn't happened before. For several weeks, I worked to be free of this smoking habit. And as often, the case received strength but had to engage my will over and over again to finally break free.

My journey was one of wonder—seeing all God's interventions—and worry, seeing all the antics of my children and myself play out. Mind you, I was trying to walk the walk, but I often didn't know or understand what exactly I was doing. Trusting Him became my hue and cry.

One early January, I prayed a prayer that seemed so right: "Whatever is between You (Lord) and me that is keeping me from growing closer to You, please remove it." Little did I know what was to come for me. Now I can say it was an answer to that prayer, but while I was going through it, I totally lost my way.

This was necessary to uncover my childhood, particularly the dark side, so that I might be rid of the many misconceptions I had about God. Most of these were born of the cult influences that lingered even into the reality of my relationship with the Lord. Needing to be purged and broken off me, separating my parents from my image of God. Separating the church image from my image of God. Becoming more childlike in relating to Him.

During the height of the process, I came to a place where I could not hold on to my relationship with Him. I began to question Him and slid into a place of not believing. Now I understand better how that served to clear out a lot of the contamination and renew a right heart in me.

And later there was this.

I had a brush with a cult-like Christian leading an active member in a charismatic prayer group. One of the leaders began another group who was following a teacher professing to have a new way to follow the Lord. It was one of total submission to the leader, sound familiar? Yes, because it was just as the cult leader of my childhood demanded. Fortunately, the group began to break up, and at one point when I was struggling, the Lord showed me this was error and to get away from It. I believe that replication was helpful in setting me free from all those misunderstandings about who God really is and isn't.

There was also this at the point when I first began to sink into the darkness of recall, and I cried out to God; it truly seemed as if He walked out and closed the door behind Him. The time when I needed Him most. Very difficult to understand; not until much later did I have any idea what had happened. C. S. Lewis had a similar experience when his wife died. It helped to know someone who I recognized as a devout follower of Christ shared this kind of reality. Later I came to realize this was not really true; He never leaves us or forsakes us. The sense of His presence may not always be with us, but He is surely there.

As I traveled this painful path, I came to a place where I completely lost my way with the Lord. I couldn't hold on after many years of suffering and torment; I didn't think He even existed. In the beginning of this uncovering, I cried out to God for help, relief—He wasn't there, and the help did not come.

Job of the Bible in chapter 30 describes it well: "…terrors have turned upon me, my life is poured out within me, the days of affliction have gripped me, my bones are pierced with aching. God has cast me into the mire. I cry to you, Lord, and you do not answer me."

It took a long time to understand, but now I can tell you if He had rescued me from this pit prematurely, what needed to be done to heal me, deliver me from evil, and set me free would not have taken place. We could not shortcut the process any more than the surgeon would stop in the middle of heart surgery, after having repaired only a portion of the problem, and sew the patient up.

Now also, I know things about the Lord and suffering that otherwise I would not comprehend. And when I am called, I can sit or stand with someone who is in very deep pain.

> He reached from on high He took me, He
> drew me out of many waters. He delivered me
> from my strong enemy. He brought me forth also
> into a large place. (Psalm 18:16–19 NLT)

In 1995, I came into a large open place in the Lord. There's no other way to describe it. But there I found a peace I had never experienced before—a joy I had never experienced before—and the Lord just keeps taking me further and deeper and higher; but now it is in Him, not in the dark past.

I would be remiss if I didn't tell you about some post-process works of God. I became aware that I was living out the anger—under the surface of my reactions was this fury, anger, and when anything scratched my surface, this anger burst out and I wrangled with God. My attitude was He owed me.

Well two things occurred: first He took me from *why me* to *why not me*. I eventually had enough health and strength to really look at what others have to suffer. You can always find people worse off than you. And you don't have to look far. Why should I feel entitled to things better than those who are caught innocently in the sex slave trade, or the street children, or others caught between bullets on the streets of many towns and cities in this world—to name three groups of people more unfortunate than me.

Another thing God did for me was as I pulled up to a stop sign in a familiar neighborhood here in my home town—and before I could leave that stopped place—He asked me if I wanted to continue being angry, or if I felt like giving it up. I realized in a flash what I had been doing and, on that spot, repented and let the anger go.

And the last thing was the forgiveness. I forgave my parents and got back, in my memory and heart, my good Papa and my good mama. Forgiving my aunt and the other perps was a little more difficult, but God's grace makes all things possible. I take no credit. I would still be flinging that "righteous" anger around in my life if it weren't for His grace, His work in my soul and my heart.

Now acknowledging the abandonment issue. I came to realize Jesus knew abandonment of friends, but He also knew what it was like to have His Father forsake Him. I believe that Jesus went with each one of us to our places of pain when He went to the cross. We enter in with Him, but He also enters in with us.

The last threshold I have to cross—and I am mostly there—is why didn't the Lord stop the abuse, rescue me? All I can tell you now is first of all, He made It possible for me to split—to dissociate until I was an adult much more able to cope. Some things are more than we can know or understand here, but I know when we are with Him, we will know and understand.

And in the meantime, I can trust Him because I know His character and trust that He is completely good. Some places in us need a very personal special touch from Him. Nothing else will do, and I know He has touched into this place of questioning in a very personal way; so while I don't understand, I don't suffer with that question anymore.

Following is an entry I made in my journal on November 13, 2001.

> The pain and terror of my life has left seemingly indelible scars across my soul. I am undone by them. They've produced a crisis of faith for me here over 15 years after the discovery of the 'awful stuff' as I have come to call it.
>
> While there were several places like this over the years, all have been faced, and God has delivered and deeply healed in every case. So I can truly say all is well with my soul as I write this on December 13, 2020.

I am now able to say I am who I am today, in large part because of all that I have come through and how God has used it. He has and will use it for good purposes in my life and in the lives of others.

I was betrayed and forsaken and abused, tortured by my parents and others. I felt forsaken by God. While I felt forsaken, He brought me through the suffering—my personal hell to His Resurrection Life.

Romans 8:17 (NLT) says it so well, "And if we are His children then we are His heirs also heirs of God and fellow heirs with Christ (sharing His inheritance with Him), only we must share His suffering if we are to share His glory."

I can honestly say—without reservation, without hesitation, and with a full heart—that now I am crazy in love with Jesus, He is everything to me.

Am I always doing the best thing or saying the right thing? No! Do I always *feel* His presence? No! But I know, beyond a shadow of a doubt, He is with me and He always has been and He always will be.

In his first letter to the Thessalonians (NLT), Paul wrote, "Faithful is He who calls you (to Himself) and utterly trustworthy. And He will also do it fulfill His call by hollowing and keeping you."

On that note of keeping, let me explain:

There are times when I feel deep reverence and awe for my Lord; other times, I am joy-filled with Him. But there are still those times, only they are even better than when I was young, when I recognize He is my best friend.

At the risk of insulting some sensibilities or shaking your theology, let me tell you of a recent time with my friend. I was talking to Him, and I heard in my spirit, *Victoria, you are a keeper.*

I replied, "Lord, you are a keeper."

He is my keeper; He kept me throughout my life, in my doubts, my rebellion, my rejection of Him, my denial of Him, my pain, grief, and mistrust. When I was sure He had forsaken me; forgotten me; and finally, when I was sure He didn't even exist, He kept me with His great keeping power—His great faithfulness.

Isaiah 49:14–16 (NIV) states, "But Zion said, 'The Lord has forsaken me and my Lord has forgotten me.' Can a woman forget her nursing child and not have compassion on the fruit of her womb? Surely they may forget yet I will not forget you. Behold, I have indelibly imprinted you on the palms of each of My hands."

Following are some scriptures that speak to me about what happened to me:

> How long will you hide your face from me?
> How long must I lay up cares withing me and
> have sorrow in my heart day after day? Consider
> and answer me, O Lord my God, lighten the eye
> of my faith to behold your face in pitchlike dark-

ness lest I sleep the sleep of death. But I have trusted Your mercy and loving kindness; my heart shall rejoice in Your salvation, I will sing to the Lord because He has dealt bountifully with me. (Psalm 13 NIV)

For the Lord has ransomed and redeemed him from the hand of him who was too strong for him. For I will turn their mourning into joy and will comfort them and make them rejoice after their sorrow and my people will be satisfied with my goodness says the Lord. (Jeremiah 31 ESV)

Yes, I am satisfied with His goodness.

But mostly, I am in love with Him.

A writing:

All the Christian life behaviors—church attendance; thanksgiving; worship and praise; reading; studying; applying and meditating on the Word of God, the Bible; receiving good teaching; praying and interceding; fellowship with others; fasting; water baptism and Holy Spirit baptism—are important, even necessary, practices of the Christian life. These help us develop spiritually.

Of course, the gifts are vital, and the fruits are God's work. More importantly, all of this is to help make it possible to go through death, the Crucible to which all of us are called.

Job is probably one of the most significant books in the Bible. We cannot change ourselves—the work of God is to conform us to His Beloved Son in our very essence. Guess what: this requires some Crucible work. We are far from Christ in ourselves even though He indwells us. He wants to live in and through us, decreasing us so that He may increase. Developing His character in us so we become more like Him has nothing to do with us and everything to do with Him.

You must go through your personal Crucible; that is what is required of you. God does all the sanctifying, and you simply stand still and let Him be God.

Somewhere along the way, you will realize what a loving work it is; and when you do, deep will call unto deep with Him in ways that would never have been possible without the crucible work being done in your life.

Victoria M.

Victoria M.

My daughter wrote the following:

It is difficult for me to convey how much suffering and pain my mother endured throughout her experiences and the residual effects from that. I am continually in awe of how she has faced, dealt with, and overcome many of the issues that were put upon her. Especially that she has learned to take care of herself, to trust her own instincts and boundaries, and to respect and honor herself. At least, that is what I observe.

As far as my experience, I have somewhat detached myself from the experience and process. It is also difficult for me to imagine my mother suffering as much as she has. So I believe my defense mechanisms, namely suppression, have come into play. Also selfishly, I want my mother to be who she was born to be and meant to be and who she really is: a warm, intelligent, kind, perfect person in many ways. I don't want anything else to rob her from this, who she truly is. This is why I may have trouble communicating or thinking about her past and how much of her childhood was robbed.

My therapist, D. Miller, wrote the following:

Victoria is a miracle.

I remember when I first saw her as a client: she was so traumatized and burdened that she would sit with her back toward me as she began to reveal and remember more and more about the atrocities that happened to her as a child. Her family was involved with a group that saw children as adult's property or playthings. Her family was one that put a lot of effort into looking like pillars of society on the outside so no one would suspect the awful things that were being done in secret. I guess families of pedophiles and child pornographers are experts at hiding the truth.

Remembering for Victoria meant feeling crazy too. How could those nice people that other people saw in the day time be the same ones that let her be so used at night. The truth came out slowly and painfully, but as it says in the Bible, "know the truth and the truth will set you free." And as she told her story, Victoria did start to become free. All those waves of fear or shame or terror that would roll over her at the most unexpected times were now tied to truth. All the night terrors, confusion, and pain now made sense.

Victoria also had to struggle so much with her view of God. Not only did she have the common questions of how could a good God let these awful things happen to children, but her parents' group were also into mind control as a way to intimidate and control kids. The group wanted the children to only be loyal to the group, so they purposely contaminated their view of God. They would tell her God wanted these things to happen to her and would also dress someone up as Jesus, who would then molest her.

They also did this with policemen, firemen, teachers, or anyone else a child might go to for help. Additionally, her family took great pride in being good Catholics. It would be a long struggle for Victoria to really be able to trust God.

Victoria remembered being subjected to awful physical, emotional, and sexual abuse. She was also subjected to torture and mind control. She was taught black was white and white was black. She was betrayed by those who were supposed to love her and protect her. She spent countless years working through deep emotional and physical pain, and the miracle is she did not give up.

She looked for truth wherever she could find it and clung to the hope that she would be healed. She and I cried together and talked together and, at times, even laughed together. I walked with her through the memories, helped try to distinguish the difference between physical pain and body memories, and helped her see the "true God" and "real Jesus."

Victoria's courage inspired me, her perseverance awed me, her seeking God humbled me, and I count it an honor to have walked with her on much of her healing path. Yes, working with—and loving—Victoria has been not only a chance to witness God's healing in action but has also let me see a miracle!

CPSIA information can be obtained
at www.ICGtesting.com
Printed in the USA
FSHW010115021221
86627FS

9 781098 097226